ORCHARDS

A Study Of The
Fruit Of The Spirit

Jason Root

Endorsements

"Jason Root's book provides a fresh look at a familiar topic. Since he comes from a military and not ministerial background Jason brings newly harvested illustrations and practical insights in the nine aspects of the Fruit of the Spirit listed in Galatians 5:22-23. Much needed and very helpful."

Bob Russell

Retired Senior Pastor, Southeast Christian Church

40 years of Preaching and Pastoral ministry has presented many opportunities to read, study and teach about the Fruit of the Spirit. Jason has written the most practical and engaging study on this subject that I have ever read! His knowledge of scripture combined with life experience creates the perfect material to weave together a study that reads more like a narrative than a traditional Bible Study. His scriptural insight and practical application of scripture followed by on point reflection questions makes this a perfect study for small groups or individual study that will keep the student engaged from beginning to end. Jason's brilliant writing ability is the glue that holds this work together and makes it a joy to read. Good work, Jason!

Jeff Noel, M.Div

Lead Pastor, Grace Heartland Church
Elizabethtown, KY

I came to the conclusion many years ago that the truest sign of being "filled with the Spirit" is the evidence of the fruit of the Holy Spirit from Paul's writings in Galatians 5:23-23.

In his new book, Orchards, Jason Root makes this even more abundantly clear as he writes about the fruit of the Spirit in such an insightful and understandable way. This is a must-read for new believers and seasoned followers of Christ as well!

Shannon McCubbins

Senior Pastor, Mount Moriah Baptist Church

"Thirty years ago my then girlfriend sat under a tree in the rolling hills of Shaker Village, Kentucky reading in John's gospel and contemplating how God was calling her to use her life. It was there that she first discovered Jesus' words: "You did not choose me but I chose you and appointed you that you should go and bear fruit and that your fruit should abide . . ." (15:16). It is an explanation of this spiritual fruit that Jason Root points us to in *Orchards*. It is a work of love and prayer and faith that points us to hope. Hope firmly rooted in Jesus.

I have the joy of knowing Jason personally and of watching him wrestle through the writing, editing and rewriting of this work. And, joyfully, to know that he's led it chapter by chapter in a small group setting to help refine it even more. Jason writes from an anguish of the heart, from wrestling with God, and from joy found by bearing fruit, fruit that will abide."

Daryl Pepper, Ph.D.

Pastor of Missions, Grace Heartland Church

Lord God, let us be one with you, so that we may bear much fruit. Let us serve others, see Your goodness in the land of the living, and let others see it fully in us. Amen.

Orchards

A Study Of The Fruit Of The Spirit

Jason Root

ISBN: 978-1-66787-592-7

All Scripture references use the NIV version of the Bible unless otherwise noted.

Permission was given by all persons mentioned by name in the book.

"But the fruit of the Spirit is love, joy, peace, patience, kindness, goodness, faithfulness, gentleness and self-control. Against such things there is no law."

Galatians 5: 22-23

Table of Contents

CHAPTER I

Introduction

But the wisdom that comes from heaven is first of all pure;
then peace-loving, considerate, submissive, full of mercy
and good fruit, impartial and sincere.

James 3:17

THE COMMON PLACE THINGS IN OUR LIVES CAN EASILY BE OVER-looked and misunderstood. Whether it is electricity or running water, we can easily lose the wonder that surrounds each of them and what they bring into our lives. Another great example of this is fruit. It is such an easy thing to take for granted because it is so common. Whether summer or winter we can find virtually any kind of fruit in our local grocery stores. The simple fact that we can get quality, affordable strawberries in the middle of winter is nothing short of a miracle.

Various bananas, grapes, watermelons, raspberries and blueberries fill our shelves in season and out. In the grocery I frequent, there are close to a dozen varieties of apples alone. It looks easy because the fruit is routinely available, but that sense can be deceiving.

I moved into my new neighborhood about ten years ago. As part of the process of clearing the land the entire forest that filled the property was completely reduced and flattened. I wasn't happy about all of the trees being cut down, but I understood why it had to happen given the effect that new buildings tend to have on trees located near them.

Even so, the area behind my house included a small strip of land that was cleared but was undeveloped. It had some rock checks on it to keep erosion from getting out of control but not much else.

After a couple of years, I decided to start planting things in that cleared strip - even though I didn't own the land. In the fall when plants would go on sale I would go and pick up a variety of things to bring home. Over the years, I have planted trees, shrubs and wild flowers. Every time I sit on my back porch I look at that land; so, why wouldn't I invest in it?

The first trip to Lowe's to do this was a memorable one. The tree that caught my eye was a beautiful six foot tall green apple tree. When I saw it, two crazy scenarios popped into my head as I imagined this apple tree growing into maturity.

The first of which was that I would be like some benevolent Disney character handing out apples to the various animals of the forest. The deer would come and feed on the apples, then tell all of their friends about what a wonderful man that lives in that one house. Sure, it could happen.

The darker scenario was that it could be an emergency food source in case of a zombie apocalypse. Yes, this was during the height of popularity of the AMC show – *The Walking Dead*. Therefore, in my mind at least, the other use would be as a vital piece of the food puzzle that would sustain us in case of that doomsday scenario. It was one of the two, or maybe even both? (And no, you don't realize just how strange those two scenarios sound until you type it out on paper. At this point I'm shaking my own head.)

Perhaps the most realistic thing I really could expect was to get enough apples to bake a pie. At this point in my journey, that smaller goal would be amazing. The tree is now on its fifth season and I have yet to get a single apple. Not one. Not a single one.

One year all of the blooms were overwhelmed by ants. Another year a really late frost completely destroyed all of the blooms. The leaves never look quite right and tend to fall early each year making me wonder if the tree will even survive to the next.

I've given the tree fertilizer. I've done things to protect and strengthen the leaves. I've watched videos. I've read articles. I am also happy to be patient with the tree and give it time. The old saying that my father taught me – a year to sleep, a year to creep, and a year to leap - told me that it might be year three before I see any significant growth or fruit on the tree. I could even welcome a few small apples. Maybe it just isn't ready for big apples yet? But nothing?

Clearly there is something about producing fruit that makes it a lot harder than the grocery store makes it out to be.

In a very similar way, when I listen to sermons about the Fruit of the Spirit there is a simplicity about the way it comes about in our lives. This is an understandable conclusion based upon a quick reading of scripture.

> **John 15:5-8 (ESV)** - "I am the vine; you are the branches. Whoever abides in me and I in him, he it is that bears much fruit, for apart from me you can do nothing. If anyone does not abide in me he is thrown away like a branch and withers; and the branches are gathered, thrown into the fire, and burned. If you abide in me, and my words abide in you, ask whatever you wish, and it will be done for you. By this my Father is glorified, that you bear much fruit and so prove to be my disciples."

It seems so simple. Just abide in Him, and you will produce fruit. The problem with that view is that either abiding is a lot tougher than we expect it, or something is happening in the process that is stealing this precious fruit away from us before it can be used for the benefit of our neighbors and ourselves.

Maybe it is as the beautiful bride urges in the second chapter of Song of Solomon, "Catch the foxes for us, the little foxes that are ruining the vineyards, while our vineyards are in bloom." What little fox is out there stealing our fruit? What is ruining the harvest before it even begins? It has never been more important for us to powerfully and effectively partner with God to produce this fruit, so it is imperative that we thoughtfully consider this subject.

This book is going to look at each aspect of the Fruit of the Spirit – love, joy, peace, patience, kindness, goodness, faithfulness, gentleness, self-control – and then what it takes to abide well with God, in an effort to understand what we can do to be effective in this area of our Christian life. Each chapter will begin with a Scripture as a starting point, and we will walk through each aspect of the Fruit of the Spirit from there. There is life and light at the end of this journey if we can get it right.

To highlight the possibilities, let's consider a story that comes out of rural India. There is a man, Jadev Payeng, who grew up near a large, barren sand bar. The trees were harvested from it which made it vulnerable to erosion and the effects of flooding. Most people saw it only as a lifeless zone. He saw it differently though. Through the years of his life, Jadev dedicated himself to reintroducing trees and plants into the area, restoring it to its natural state. Now a variety of wildlife - birds, deer, apes, rhino, elephants and even tigers can be found on this 1300+ acre forest. What was once barren and lifeless is now full of life and potential.[1]

So what does this have to do with spiritual fruit? There are two interesting things about fruit that draw us to this story.

The first interesting thing is that fruit carries the seed of itself. Break open an apple and you will see the seeds. There is potential within that one piece of fruit to produce so much more of itself. I understand it is a bit more complex than this; but if you want to be surrounded by a forest of apple trees, you could do worse than starting with handing out apples.

The second interesting thing about fruit is that the primary beneficiary of the fruit isn't the plant itself. The fruit, when consumed, sustains life and gives nourishment to bodies that can be desperate for the vitamins, carbohydrates and protein inside of it. The fruit, when the seeds are harvested and planted, can also produce gardens and forests that become shelter for all kinds of life.

Let's remember Jadev and his efforts. He intentionally sat out to make a place for life to thrive in. He planted and cared for trees that eventually grew into a forest.

Can we do the same thing with the Fruit of the Spirit?

Do you want to be surrounded by patience? Perhaps it is time to hand out some. Yes, much of it will be consumed. Some of it eventually will be planted around you and, with care, a forest of it will grow up around you.

That's just one example, but I am convinced that we can grow orchards of the best of things all around us. It will take intentionality. It will take focus. It will take help from God. Of those three, the first two belong to us. The third? Trust me when I say that God is more than eager to help us with this task.

So let's get started.

For Further Reflection...

1. What would your life look like if it was surrounded by love and joy?

2. What would your life look like if it was surrounded by peace and patience?

3. What would your life look like if it was surrounded by kindness and goodness?

4. What would your life look like if it was surrounded by faithfulness and self-control?

5. Is this a life worth fighting for?

6. Is this transformation our responsibility or God's responsibility?

Part 1
The Fruit

Galatians 5: 22-23 – "But the fruit of the Spirit is love, joy, peace, patience, kindness, goodness, faithfulness, gentleness and self-control. Against such things there is no law."

CHAPTER 2

Love

This is how God showed His love among us: He sent his one and only Son into the world that we might live through him.

1 John 4:9

HAVE YOU EVER BEEN AROUND GREAT WEALTH?

Many years ago, when my son was in elementary school, my wife, son and I visited my Dad's cousin in Fort Lauderdale, Florida. For a long time, he sold Ferraris. Pretty cool.

These cars are exquisite. The craftsmanship transcends engineering to become works of art. They were, and are, such beautiful machines. The balance, the precision, the thought that goes into even the smallest detail on each one is astounding. So many layers and details that you don't notice unless you have a guide who reveals them to you.

As we walked in for a visit and a test drive, I looked over and saw that one of the Ferraris that was in for service had a custom license plate. I laughed at the words on it. It read – Bada Bing. I chucked and said the words out loud.

Then, a strange thing happened. My son corrected me and said, "Dad, it says – Bada Bang." I looked at him, and he at me. When we looked out again at the plates we realized that we were looking at two different cars. It turned out that one guy owned both of them! That set our mind spinning. He owns TWO of them? The brake job alone on one of these vehicles is close to $10,000, and he owns two of them? How much money did he have in order to own two of them? (We found out later that he also owned a racing Porsche that had a plate – Bada Boom, so it was even more amazing!)

That kind of wealth just makes my imagination run wild. Much like the Lexus commercials that come on around Christmas time where a loving spouse apparently purchases an $80,000 car without the knowledge of the other. I remember watching one of the early versions of that commercial, leaning towards my wife and asking her how much money we would have to have in our bank account before I could buy her a surprise vehicle without her knowledge, not exactly knowing if she would like it, and it be okay? Her answer? A whole lot more than we currently had. Fair enough. So I left it at that.

Even so, after we saw the Ferraris and knew some of the back story on the owner, we couldn't help but wonder about what it would be like to have that kind of money. What would we do with that money? What would we purchase? Where we would we travel to? How would our lives be different? Who would we help with that money?

I ask that because the contrast that was fresh in my mind was something that related to my son's elementary school. At the time I was serving as the PTA President. We had just come out of what I thought was an incredibly successful fundraiser where we raised over $5,000 for the school. There were things we were going to buy for the teachers and help make the school a better place. We were so excited!

Then I heard a story on the radio about an affluent neighborhood in Seattle that raised almost $100,000 for their school through a PTA fundraiser. I was stunned. How in the world did they do that?

That kind of money once again sparked the imagination into what was possible. What would we have done with that kind of money? What improvements would we have been able to make that would have enabled our great teachers to be even better at what they did?

Encounters with great abundance makes you wonder about your life and what might be possible if you had the same thing.

Several years ago I had the privilege of hosting one of the missionaries we support out of our church in my home. Pastor Job Hyppolite-Jean runs a church and elementary school in Haiti. He does amazing work for his church and community.

When he came to visit our church with his two boys, I was proud to serve them massive amounts of food (like my giant frankenburgers) and, in general, spoil them in any way I could. They were very grateful.

I even worked it out so that each of them had their own room. That way each of them could have privacy and peace for the evening. He had mentioned to me in passing that his entire house fit into the confines of just a few of the rooms in my home, so I thought I was doing him a favor.

When I explained the sleeping arrangements, he just looked at me in a very curious way as if to say – why would we do that? Why was separating his family a good thing?

They ended up sleeping all together in one room in our finished basement. What I began to see was a togetherness within his family that, quite frankly, my family did not have. Not that my family is any more dysfunctional than any other, but we each need our own space to be sane.

I saw something in his family that made me stop. It made me wonder about the differences between our two families. I was just amazed at the level of togetherness and the closeness that his family had. What would that be like? What would a life lived like that feel like, and how would it not only affect me but everyone else I encountered? I knew that this was "wealth" of a different kind. This encounter with abundance, just like the others, made me wonder about what was possible.

There are moments like that in the Bible as well. In the history of the early Church, there is an astounding statement that produces a similar sense of awe.

> **Acts 4:32-35** – "All the believers were one in heart and mind. No one claimed that any of their possessions was their own, but they shared everything they had. With great power the apostles continued to testify to the resurrection of the Lord Jesus. *And God's grace was so powerfully at work in them all that there were no needy persons among them.* For from time to time those who owned land or houses sold them, brought the money from the sales and put it at the apostles' feet, and it was distributed to anyone who had need." *(Emphasis added).*

How is it that there was no one in need? There are strong, obvious connections to wealth in this; but if you are around people long enough, regardless of the setting, you will figure out that there are more ways to live in poverty than just not having enough money.

I have known people with incredible wealth who were lonely to the point of despair. I have known incredibly kind and warm people who struggled to put food on the table. For that matter, I have met people who cared about their community and others, yet were spiritually dead on the inside. Their hearts yearned to have the God shaped hole filled, but they weren't filling it with the right things so the ache remained. I had to give them credit for at least trying to fill it with good things instead of destructive ones. (We all know people who are like that. If we are honest we ARE those people from time to time.)

So how did the early Church do it? How did they live in a way that there were no needy persons among them?

That Church was closer to Jesus, the living embodiment of love, than any other in history. There were many people among them who walked personally with Jesus. They were instructed by Him, lived and breathed with Him on a daily basis. They walked the dusty and long roads with Him, they shared in the struggles, triumphs and trials of His life. That had to have a significant impact. They knew what He came to do. They knew His heart and how He loved people.

It is instructive then to go back to where Christ's ministry began to gain a sense of what they learned along the way. When Jesus went into the Temple and read from the scroll that contained the words of the prophet Isaiah, He was laying out His mission.

> **Luke 4:14-21** – "Jesus returned to Galilee in the power of the Spirit, and news about him spread through the whole countryside. He was teaching in their synagogues, and everyone praised him. He went to Nazareth, where he had been brought up, and on the Sabbath day he went into the synagogue, as was his custom. He stood up to read, and the scroll of the prophet Isaiah was handed to him. Unrolling it, he found the place where it is written:

> 'The Spirit of the LORD is on me, because he has anointed me to proclaim good news to the poor. He has sent me to proclaim freedom for the prisoners and recovery of sight for the blind, to set the oppressed free, to proclaim the year of the LORD's favor.'

> Then he rolled up the scroll, gave it back to the attendant and sat down. The eyes of everyone in the synagogue were fastened on him. He began by saying to them, 'Today this scripture is fulfilled in your hearing.'"

It is interesting to follow the two parallels in these cases. Jesus, love personified, had just returned in the power of the Spirit, and His first declaration was to address poverty. The early Church in Acts had just been filled with the Holy Spirit and were living life in that power. What was the result?

There were no needy persons among them.

There are as many ways to live in abundance as there are ways to live in need. Those are just opposites of each other. There is something deeper that must be addressed in all of this.

We begin to understand that beyond abundance and need is the goal to deal with a deeper issue: poverty. Poverty - either spiritual, physical or environmental - can be present in abundance and need. Many people have struggled over the years to define and to corral this destructive force, but we see here something that cries out to be understood.

Poverty is being removed, either in reality or by perception, from the law of sowing and reaping.

Repeatedly, the Bible uses this idea of sowing and reaping to explain physical and spiritual processes in our lives.[2] If we plant good seeds, we will reap a good harvest. If we plant bad seeds, we will reap a bad harvest. You sow and you reap.

We should not be able to plant an apple, and expect to grow an orange, right? In the same way, we should not be able plant weeds and expect to produce a harvest of flowers.

Yet in our lives we see this; that there is something in the world that is profoundly broken. In Ecclesiastes 8:14 the writer observes, "There is something else meaningless that occurs on earth: the righteous get what the wicked deserve, and the wicked who get what the righteous deserve"

In an eternal sense, yes, we will reap what we sow.

> **Galatians 6:7-10** – "Do not be deceived: God cannot be mocked. A man reaps what he sows. Whoever sows to please their flesh, from the flesh will reap destruction; whoever sows to please the Spirit will reap eternal life. Let us not become weary in doing good, for at the proper time we will reap a harvest if we do not give up. Therefore, as we have opportunity, let us do good to all people, especially to those who belong to the family of believers."

God will make all things right, but we have an opportunity as believers to bring His kingdom into the present. We pray, "Your kingdom come, Your will be done, on earth as it is in Heaven" (Matthew 6:10) This is part of our mission. This is part of how we love others.

Have you ever seen or been in a relationship that, despite doing all the right things you can, never transforms into something better? Poverty.

Have you ever been in a situation that no matter how hard and diligently you work, you never seem to be able to get ahead in your bills? Poverty.

Have you ever done everything you ever could to measure up and get the approval of God, only to fall short? Poverty.

Jesus came to end poverty in all of its forms.

There are places in this world where no matter how hard one tries, the systematic corruption makes it nearly impossible for anyone to get ahead. That kind of forced poverty is very real.

There are also mindsets that chain people in those systems so that even if the environment changes, they are still trapped and believe that nothing they can ever do will change their circumstances. Sometimes it is a combination of both factors and other hardships.

There are stories about how elephants were broken and trained that is useful as an analogy. As a juvenile an elephant was tied to a stake. It struggles and pulls with all of its might for a time, but because it is small, it cannot break free and eventually it is broken mentally. It is mentally chained to the point that even as it grows into a powerful adult it will not challenge the stake because it knows in its heart that it cannot do it. That is a perceived reality, but powerful nonetheless, and twice as tragic. Power perceived is power achieved.

And that spiritual poverty where you believe that nothing you could ever do will be able to measure up to God's standard? That isn't a perception. That is reality. There is no amount of good deeds or no amount of money you could ever give that would allow you to measure up to God's standard of Holiness.

That's why Jesus came.

> **Luke 4:18-19** - "The Spirit of the LORD is on me, because he has anointed me to proclaim good news to the poor. He has sent me to proclaim freedom for the prisoners and recovery of sight for the blind, to set the oppressed free, to proclaim the year of the LORD's favor."

At its heart, the ministry of Jesus came to love people, and as an extension, end poverty. As He indicated by reading the prophetic passages in Isaiah, He came to give us good news. He came to set the prisoner and oppressed free. Through the work He did on the cross, Jesus broke the back of poverty, and with the power of the Holy Spirit, we now get to carry on that ministry and seek to make our world as it is in Heaven.

As a contrast, imagine the time before sin in the Garden of Eden. Can you picture what it was like for Adam and Eve to have a perfect relationship between what they put effort into and the results they achieved, no matter what area of their lives they focused on? How amazing would that be if that was restored in our lives today!

So how do we begin? Where do we start?

It is easy to look at our lives through the lens of what we don't have. To see areas in our lives where there is poverty. I'm not saying that it is a bad thing to recognize where you have poverty in your life. Far from it. Those should be areas that we focus on during prayer and look for ways to gain freedom. However, if we are to break free of poverty as a church and a people, we really need to ask ourselves a different question. Where do we have abundance?

It may be that you have great monetary wealth. More than just giving money to those who are in immediate need, can you teach those around you how that money was made and help them to gain wealth for themselves? Can you help others realize that even though they came from need they can live a life of prosperity and generosity?

It may be that you have a great marriage. More than just giving a room for someone to stay in case of a marriage breakdown, can you help teach others about what it takes to have a great marriage? Can you help others realize that even though they come from a family with a history of divorce, they can have a healthy marriage themselves?

For us to break the back of poverty, we all have to give out of the abundance we have. In no way does this mean we have to be perfect in any of that area. Mistakes that we make along the way, when put in their proper perspective, help to strengthen and encourage those we help.

One of the great unspoken sins of the modern Church (and I am speaking to all of us as believers rather than to the corporate leadership) is that we have not fought for others in terms of our own abundance.

There is a moment in the history of Israel where the Twelve Tribes are finally moving into the Promised Land, ready to cross the Jordan River and possess what God promised them. It is tempting to think, especially in light of the way that God showed Himself in power by causing the Jordan River to back up (see Joshua 3), that all of the Promised Land was past the Jordan River, but it wasn't!

The Reubenites, the Gadites, and the half tribe of Manasseh were given land that was on the near side of the Jordan. Moses was clear with them that even if they were to possess this land they would be sinning if they did not go forward and fight for the rest of the land with their people.

> **Numbers 32:20-24** – "Then Moses said to them, "If you will do this-if you will arm yourselves before the LORD for battle and if all of you who are armed cross over the Jordan before the LORD until he has driven his enemies out before him- then when the land is subdued before the LORD, you may return and be free from your obligation to the LORD and to Israel. And this land will be your possession before the LORD. "But if you fail to do this, you will be sinning against the LORD; and you may be sure that your sin will find you out. Build cities for your women and children, and pens for your flocks, but do what you have promised." "

They were to fight for the prosperity of others even though they had reached a place of prosperity themselves.

Can you imagine if they had looked at Moses and said, "Nope, we're good. We've got good land and good places to live. That doesn't really look all that safe over there. You go on ahead. We'll be posting inspirational pictures and quotes on Instagram for you though! Good luck!"?

Especially in light of how God seemed to interact with His people in the Old Testament, that would not have ended well. Our actions must start with prayer and then be followed up with our personal interaction with the poverty we encounter. We must fight!

In many ways, this is where we find ourselves today. We are separated and sometimes miserable. Stuck in pockets of partial abundance, afraid to step out and fight for someone else's prosperity because we fear it will end ours, when actually the opposite is true.

Great loving and faith filled families and marriages are out there. Great business that run with integrity and honor are out there. Communities that disperse justice to all equally are out there.

The answers may not be where we think. The wisdom to gain that abundance may offend us on many levels. Are we to learn from those in abundance or rely to on our own knowledge that has us wallowing in need? It is one of the great pitfalls of missionary work, especially from the United States, to believe that we have all of the answers when we travel to another country to do work.

The best way this can be done is to have a mindset where we are there to share in the abundance we have and learn from the abundance they have. William Butler Yeats says, "Education is not the filling of a pail, but the lighting of a fire." In each place we travel in this world, we have an opportunity to share the "fire" that God has given us, to share our prosperity with those who may not look like us, talk like us, or even believe the customs we do. In doing so, they have an opportunity to do the same for us.

The abundance and lack of need in the early Church didn't come from uniformity. That is a false path. It came from diversity and unity. We simply cannot do this alone. This diversity and unity in Christ brought with it pockets of abundance that could be shared until, as it says in Acts 4, "there were no needy persons among them."

When done right, it is messy and glorious all at the same time. The disciples were a group of misfits who most likely would have never associated with each other outside of the passion to follow Jesus. Healthy churches today see the same thing reflected in the people who worship there. Many different races, political parties, economic backgrounds; all brought together because of a passion to follow Christ.

When Paul writes in Romans 8:32 – "He who did not spare his own Son, but gave Him up for us all – how will He not also, along with Him, graciously give us all things?" it is tempting to think that God will give us all things from His hand directly to ours. I don't believe that is the case. I believe He gives "all things" into the hands of many, then it is up to us to share.

When Jesus prayed in John 17:20-21 – "My prayer is not for them alone. I pray also for those who will believe in me through their message, that all of them may be one, Father, just as you are in me and I am in you. May they also be in us so that the world may believe that you have sent me." This prayer is a great call for unity in Christ. Bringing those two thoughts together, from a strategic perspective, if you thought that unity was vital to the body of Christ, would you give "all things" to one group that all looked alike and thought alike, or would you spread those blessings out to many groups? Would you spread them out so that as they learned to love each other they would be blessed with ever greater measures of prosperity and life?

It isn't enough to sit on the sidelines. Edmond Burke says "the only thing necessary for the triumph of evil is for good men to do nothing." Make no doubt about it, there are forces in this world who are fighting for division and working to keep these systems in place. Sitting still is the same as fighting for the other side.[3]

This happens often because we don't recognize the symptoms in ourselves. As an example, just because you have money doesn't mean you don't have a poverty mindset. Wealth with a poverty mindset is greed. It is a false path that states that your prosperity means less for me. Jesus calls us to a higher path.

> **Matthew 22:34-40** – "Hearing that Jesus had silenced the Sadducees, the Pharisees got together. One of them,

an expert in the law, tested him with this question: 'Teacher, which is the greatest commandment in the Law?' Jesus replied: "'Love the LORD your God with all your heart and with all your soul and with all your mind.' This is the first and greatest commandment. And the second is like it: 'Love your neighbor as yourself.' All the Law and the Prophets hang on these two commandments.'"

Loving your neighbor as yourself, in part, means not becoming comfortable in your abundance while others are stuck in poverty.

This is not easy. Loving well will take us out of our comfort zones and cause us to associate with people who may make us squirm. They may not look like us, think like us, or even be in the same political party, but just like the Israelites getting ready to cross the Jordan river, we have a question before us. Will we will stay where we perceive it is safe, or will we go fight for our brothers and sisters in need? If we fight we might just end their poverty and our own at the same time.

What will your response be?

For Further Reflection...

1. What would your life look like if you were able to make gains in every area (work, relationships, finances, etc.) in which you decided to put effort?

2. Where do you start?

3. Where do you have need?

4. Where can you go to seek wisdom?

5. Where do you have abundance?

6. How can you bless others with your abundance?

7. How can this aspect of the fruit of the spirit (Love) be stolen?

Loving others out of our abundance is critical to the work Jesus calls us to do in this world. It crosses economic, racial, and social boundaries, but it isn't easy. Loving well will be one of the highest and hardest mountains you will ever climb in your life.

How will we ever find the strength to do such a task?

It's almost as if it is going to take something else along the way to be able to accomplish the hard work that God has called us to do. It's almost as if we will need...

Joy

*You have made known to me the paths of life; you will fill
me with joy in your presence.*

Acts 2:28

Iᶠ YOU WERE ABLE TO GO BACK IN TIME TO LOOK AT ME IN HIGH
school and follow my athletic accomplishments (anyone who played with
me during that time is already laughing), you wouldn't find many. I had enough
talent and physical skills to be good at the high school level. I wasn't naturally
strong or fast, but I was close to six foot, moderately strong, and was generally
talented enough to play high school sports.

So what was missing? Probably more than a few things. After college,
I joined the Army as an officer. I always laughed when some of my soldiers
would ask me if I played football at Ohio State. I would tell them that I was
only missing five things or I would have played. Size, speed, strength, skill and
heart for the game. If I had just those five little things, Eddie George would
have been riding the pine and I would have had that Heisman. Just little things.

When I look back on my life and my time spent in high school sports, there truly is one important thing missing when I compare it to the really successful things I have had in my life: joy.

I liked the idea of playing football more than I really actually enjoyed the playing the game. Consequently, I never gave it my heart. I never was willing to work for it. I never really improved, never made gains; and as a result, never really tasted the same thrill of victory and joy that others experienced. Something was missing, but I didn't know what it was.

Later, as a cadet at Ohio State I found a home. I found a goal and a path to the purpose for part of my life. I found something that I was willing to sacrifice and work really hard for. I found joy.

In December of 1993, I was chosen to go to Air Assault School at Camp Gruber, Oklahoma. It was a difficult school that had a reputation of failing close to a third of each class. I trained hard to be ready. The most elite cadets that I looked up to had both Airborne and Air Assault Qualification wings upon their chest. I had been to Airborne School earlier that summer, and now I had my next goal in sight. I wanted to be elite and to be counted among the best of my class.

What is funny is that as I was preparing for the school, somehow I had convinced myself that Oklahoma is in the south (it is from Columbus, Ohio so I was correct in that sense) and that it would be warm there. That part about "warm" is the really questionable idea. (Now anyone who is familiar with Oklahoma is laughing.)

A vivid moment of understanding came to me as I boarded the plane to Oklahoma. I remembered one of the previous weekend's games in the NFL. One of those games featured the Miami Dolphins playing the Dallas Cowboys in Dallas during heavy snowfall. They had enough snow that they were making snow angels after scoring touchdowns. It was a thrilling finish punctuated by Leon Lett sliding into a blocked kick that ended up giving the Dolphins another try at a winning field goal. Strange and exciting game, but in all of that it suddenly dawned upon me that all of Oklahoma is NORTH of Dallas. Well north. A long way north.

It might not be as warm as I thought.

Ready or not, I reported in for the training. We all had a restless night of sleep waiting for the first day of training, which at the time they called Zero Day. We came out for PT (Physical fitness Training) and prepared ourselves mentally for the trial to come.

The wind was howling and it wasn't much above the low 40's. A rain came through the night before leaving about a quarter inch of standing water on the ground. We all were trying to stay out of the water as much as possible. It was a losing battle, and then we got down to do sit ups.

To this day I have never heard a group yell out in discomfort as much as we did that day. (And that is a nice way of saying it.) I still am not sure which was worse; putting my back down in the ice cold water that was on the ground, or coming out of the water and then having the freezing wind hit my back. Our instructors would pause us either in the up or down position until we got the full effect of each. It was absolute misery.

Was I going to give up? Nope.

I wanted to rappel from helicopters (to this day one of the most thrilling things I have ever done). I wanted those wings and to be elite. There was no way I was going to let that moment get in the way.

It is a lesson that has stuck with me over the years about what I am willing to commit myself to, and one that I have tried to pass along to my son.

Early in his life, my son Gavin played a number of sports. He played a lot of soccer, and was quite good at it. He enjoyed it but not enough that he really wanted to work at it. He even played football for a season. It was all I could do to even get him to finish the season. I knew that wasn't his sport.

Then there was basketball. That became his passion. That became his great love. He works harder at that game than anyone I know. He finds joy in the game that most people never get to feel. It allows him to sacrifice and fight through tough times. It is a vehicle that continues to shape his life. I am very proud of him.

There is a relationship between the difficult God given tasks in our lives, our ability to sustain hard work, and the joy we experience. This isn't just our occupation. This applies to our roles as parents, spouses, children and disciples. Joy is centered on the presence of God, so as many flavors of difficult, God given work that are in front of us, there are as many flavors of joy for us to experience. Sometimes it is found in our profession and sometimes it is found in the way we care and love each other.

There are places in the Bible where you can see the relationship between the difficult tasks of the moment, the strength needed to complete them, and the joy experienced. One clear example of this is in the book of Nehemiah, which is primarily about the rebuilding of the walls of Jerusalem.

When the Israelites came back after exile to Jerusalem they found the walls broken and the gates burned. To rebuild them was going to be an enormous undertaking. So much so that the task was not fully accomplished until Nehemiah was called to take up the work. Nehemiah understood the relationship between the God given work and the joy people would experience to sustain them.

> **Nehemiah 8:10** – "Nehemiah said, 'Go and enjoy choice food and sweet drinks, and send some to those who have nothing prepared. This day is holy to our Lord. Do not grieve, for *the joy of the Lord is your strength.*'" (*Emphasis added*).

When we work that in alignment with the purpose that God has for our lives, it produces joy. This is in contrast to happiness, which is temporary and can actually be aligned in such a way that it is counter to the purposes of God in our lives.

Joy is different. There is something down inside that is fed when we move forward with the work that God has given us to do in our lives. It sustains us in difficulty and trial. The opportunity I had to work hard as a cadet and then as an officer in the Army, was tied to the purpose that God had for my life. It sustained me through deployments, separations, terrible conditions and danger. I was able to get through, serve and lead others well because my heart was being sustained by God through it all. It was part of my purpose at the time.

Each of us has a purpose for the season of our lives we are in. I am a firm believer that when our purpose on Earth is complete, so are our lives. So if you are reading this, you still have purpose, and you can still have joy as an outcome. This grace that God gives us to work well at the things He has given us to do is one of the greatest gifts we receive in our lives.

For each of us, it is different. I have friends who are accountants and are incredibly successful at it. Looking at numbers like they do just drains the life from me. No amount of coffee, dollars in a paycheck, or coercion could get me to be good at that. It just isn't my purpose, and consequently, I would never excel at it.

Within my own family there is even this contrast. I love to cook. The people around me think I am pretty good at it. (Or maybe they just don't want to cook themselves, you could possibly argue a bit both ways.) That said, part of why I do it is because it gives me a special joy to see someone really enjoy something I have created. I love that feeling to serve someone like that and see their face light up. Whether it is my smoked ribs, my (locally) famous spaghetti and freshly baked bread, or just a great steak on the grill, the reaction is priceless. It sustains me. It is part of my purpose.

Would anyone argue that if you want to be a good Christian you need to be able to cook well and enjoy it? No, absolutely not. My wife dislikes cooking. She can do it, but it doesn't really produce joy in her life. There are other things in her life that do, and when she does them, watch out. There is no one better. (I might be a little biased, but I ask you to grant me the point.)

Her work, when tied to the purpose God has in any one of the seasons in her life, has produced magic.

She ran a daycare center on our base in Europe. I am convinced it was part of the purpose God had in her life because of the excellence with which she did it. She later came back to teaching music; and, to see the things she was able to do with elementary and high school kids is nothing short of amazing. It is part of her purpose, and God gave her the strength through joy to do it well. Oh how her kids loved her!

There is no clearer example in this that I can give you than of Jesus Himself.

> **Hebrews 12:1-3 -** "Therefore, since we are surrounded by such a great cloud of witnesses, let us throw off everything that hinders and the sin that so easily entangles. And let us run with perseverance the race marked out for us, fixing our eyes on Jesus, the pioneer and perfecter of faith. *For the joy set before Him He endured the cross, scorning its shame, and sat down at the right hand of the throne of God.* Consider Him who endured such opposition from sinners, so that you will not grow weary and lose heart." (*Emphasis added.*)

If you know much about Christ's life you know some of the trials that He went through. He suffered and was tempted in every way that we are today; yet He had the strength not to sin or falter in any way.[4] How is that possible? The joy He was given that was associated with His purpose sustained and propelled Him throughout His life.

Depending on how specific you want to be, there are many purposes that Jesus had in His time on earth, just like we do. "He came to give us life, and have it abundantly." (John 10:10) He came to destroy the works of the devil." (1 John 3:8) He came to testify to the truth. (John 18:37) I think that even with all of those in mind it is impossible to ignore that one of the great purposes of Jesus was to redeem humanity and restore the ability to have relationship with God. This was His work on the cross. We were the joy set before Him that propelled His work and mission. Now He is the joy set before us that propels our work and mission. We get to have more of Him, and that is joy! He had to go through opposition, grief and sorrow to get to that moment on the cross. We are no different in getting to our joy.

As part of the process of writing this book I taught through the material first with a great group of people at my Church. The morning of this class proved to be very instructive on this subject and provided that last point about fighting to joy.

The day started off routinely. I had a morning appointment to drop my dog off at the groomers before going into work. Since the appointment was at 8:30 I was able to get up a little later than normal and even had time to go for a walk. As my wife left the house for work, she instinctively locked the house up, and in the process – locked me out of it. She was almost all the way to work when I called her for help. No open doors or windows and our spare key was inside, as we had failed to replace it from a visit from my mother-in-law. That was a fun phone call.

Once I did get back into the house, I was able to get back on track and went out to the car to take my dog to its appointment. I had noticed the battery was a little sluggish the day before, but didn't think anything of it. At least I didn't think anything of it until the car wouldn't start. I fumed at my carelessness and was lucky to be able to find a neighbor who could give me a jump to at least get going, but it was more drama and delay I just didn't need.

When I arrived at the groomer I began the process of getting the dog inside. My dog has a funny thing about it where I can't hand it to the groomer. He snaps at the groomer if I do that, but if I put my dog on a leash, I can hand the leash to the groomer and everything is fine. Not sure why it works, but it does. So I reached to my dog to put the leash on and realized the dog didn't have its collar on for some reason. The frustration was mounting. I tried to find a collar in my car but ended up leaning on the patience and generosity of the groomer, who happened to have an extra one.

I then hurried into work to a meeting with our Senior Commander, a two star general, on unit readiness and resiliency. In this meeting each of the various units from Fort Knox described issues they were having with drug addictions, mental health, suicide and divorce. Each of the units talked about the training and plans they had to combat the problems they faced. It felt at times like we were trying to put out a house fire with a small cup of water. It was topped off by a presentation on the local conditions on COVID 19, which were getting significantly worse at the time. The commanders and staff were upbeat, but it was not a cheery subject.

Then near the end of the meeting I got a text informing me that a friend I had known for over thirty years passed away. She had been struggling with brain cancer and early that morning lost her fight. I ducked out of the meeting and sat in my car feeling completely overwhelmed. In the worst of it, through my tears of loss for my friend, I wondered how in the world I was going to teach that evening on joy! I felt as if all of the joy I had been ripped out of me. How was I going to do this?

I began to pray. I told God I needed his help, now more than ever, to understand what was going on and to reorient myself so I could teach the subject like He wanted me to. I didn't want to fail Him on this.

I would like to tell you that it happened all at once, that I was immediately flooded with peace at the moment of my first prayer, and that I clearly saw the answer on how to get to joy, but the reality is that it was a process I had to fight through. As I went through the second half of my day, I had many chances to medicate my pain in various ways. Each of them was a temptation to look to something other than God for comfort, relief or distraction from my pain, not to mention the answer to my question. I don't always get it right, but this afternoon I did. Each time instead of leaning on some other source I went to God with my questions and my pain, and across the day He answered.

I remembered that I get tremendous joy from teaching. I began to think about the opposition that Jesus had to face to get to His joy, and now I saw clearly what was trying to stop me from getting to mine. And just like Jesus I had to fight through grief and sorrow and the opposition of sinful men. Of course, it had never occurred to me before that one of the sinful men I would have to overcome was me. Still, the more I focused on Him, the clearer the answer became. It was as if those first three verses in Hebrews 12 were a treasure map guiding me to my prize. The sideways X of the cross did indeed mark the spot. Focusing on Him brought me to the class with the answers, my purpose, and my joy.

Every joy has a fight - some great, some small. Most of the time the greatest purpose and joys come with an equally proportioned challenge. Again, using Jesus as the example, the angels sang about great joy at the birth of Jesus.

> **Luke 2:9-11** – "An angel of the Lord appeared to them, and the glory of the Lord shone around them, and they were terrified. But the angel said to them, do not be afraid. I bring you good news that will cause great joy for all the people. Today in the town of David a Savior has been born to you; He is the Messiah, the Lord."

Is there any wonder there is such joy at the birth of any child? Within a child is the possibility of purpose fulfilled, the greatness of God revealed and the possibility of the greatest of joys experienced. Great challenges await as well.

So what is your purpose in this season of your life? Young or old, if you are reading these words, God still has a purpose for you and your life. What is it?

Mark Twain said that the two most important moments in your life are when you are born, and when you find out why. There is something to that. When we tie our work to our purpose we gain the strength to do what others never could.

What task in your life can you do that others seem to struggle with in their motivation and success? Does that activity serve other people and not just yourself? Each of these are clues to what your purpose might be in this season of your life.

Each of us is unique, and the purposes we carry are equally unique; therefore it is important not to mistake our purpose for the purpose of another. That may come off as an accusation of selfishness, but there are people in my life that have incredible ministries. It can be easy for me to mistake admiring their ministry versus admiring their impact.

If I fall in love with a task, maybe because I think it has more glory than another, then I may miss my purpose altogether. I may tie myself to a task that I don't have the strength to complete. It's happened more than once in my life. Someone else's path doesn't contain the strength you need nor the joy that God intends for you.

On the path of my purpose God is waiting for me, just as He is for you.

> **Psalm 16:11** – "You make known to me the path of life; you will fill me with joy in your presence, with eternal pleasures at your right hand."

On that path is strength. On that path is blessing. On that path is joy.

For Further Reflection...

1. What is joy?

2. Is happiness bad? What role does it play in our lives?

3. How is joy related to the purpose God has for our lives?

4. Where do you find joy that others do not?

5. How can that joy be brought to serve others?

6. Why is it important to pursue purpose rather than a specific task?

7. What are the things that most typically steal or block you from your joy?

Joy sustains us in difficult moments of our lives. It helps us to do things that others will never be able to do. Finding the purpose that God has for our lives is a pursuit that we never stop, as it shifts and flows through the seasons of our lives.

Even with joy the tasks that we take on can be incredibly difficult to achieve. They require us to have solid foundation to work from. A solid platform to build our work and lives on. Those things require...

CHAPTER 4

Peace

Peace I leave with you; my peace I give you. I do not give to you as the world gives. Do not let your hearts be troubled and do not be afraid.

John 14:27

ON THE 6TH OF SEPTEMBER 2017 HURRICANE IRMA ROARED ACROSS the U.S. Virgin Islands of St. Croix, St. Thomas and St. John. The storm landed as a Category 5 hurricane and caused widespread damage to the islands and their infrastructure. Almost unbelievably, less than two weeks later Hurricane Maria would again tear through the U.S. Virgin Islands as a Category 4 storm.

The combined effect of the two hurricanes left the islands completely devastated in places. Some of the roads were impassable. The power grid was in shambles. To make things worse, a mind numbing amount of debris from buildings, plants and trees were created by the storms.

As part of the disaster response, the U.S. Army Corps of Engineers was called in to help with the recovery efforts. The recovery from major storms such as these can take years and requires shifts of teams from many government and private organizations. I felt called to go and volunteered to help with the mission near the end of May of 2018.

A day before I was to leave I came across a verse in Proverbs that just seemed to jump out of the page.

> **Proverbs 3:27** – "Do not withhold good from those to whom it is due, when it is in your power to act."

It was almost as if the verse was highlighted on the page. I just couldn't quite get away from it. Why was this passage sticking with me so much?

In many ways, it felt like a set of orders. As if to say, "Pay attention to this, Jason" I wrote the verse on the back of one of my business cards I carried in my wallet and tucked it away as something to remember for the trip ahead. I wasn't sure what it all meant, but I was eager to find out.

I left the next day and began to get oriented to the islands and my new mission. If you have never been there, the Virgin Islands are a beautiful set of islands with equally beautiful people, but there are several cultural differences you have to work through quickly. Chief among these things is the fact that they drive on the left side of the road. Suffice to say, until you get used to it, which take several weeks, you tend to have plenty of exciting moments.

The way people drive even filters down to everyday encounters. Everywhere I went I was walking on the wrong side of the hallways. I didn't realize it until I arrived, but so many of the paradigms we follow in the way we walk through offices or malls is governed by how we think about traffic laws. I had to rely on the kindness of the islanders until I got used to the lay of the land.

By the time I arrived, the debris had already been collected in various sites on the islands. What was left was the tedious process of sorting the material so it could be shipped off of the island. I couldn't quite believe it the first time I saw it. The piles just kept going and going. To put it in perspective, for just the three small islands, if you stacked all of the debris in a football field, the resulting stack would have been almost as tall as the Statue of Liberty.

Through it all I kept hearing the whispers of the Proverb that I had been sent down to the islands with.

Proverbs 3:27 – "Do not withhold good from those to whom it is due, when it is in your power to act."

As much as I tried, I just somehow knew that what I had done for my mission and the people I worked with up to that point wasn't what God had in mind for me to do. There were many good things to be sure, but that just didn't seem to be it. It just hadn't clicked yet. I hadn't found out why I had come.

Then the following Sunday I arranged to take the morning off to go to Church. I had scanned many of the websites for the Churches near my hotel and found one that seemed to fit. The St. Croix Christian Church was getting a visitor from the north.

Upon arrival, two things stood out. First, this was one of the most racially diverse church I had ever attended. Second, the way they welcomed people was warmer than almost any place I had ever been. The people were friendly and genuinely very interested in who I was and what I was doing on the island.

I was quickly introduced to Shelley Claey, who was serving with her husband as the youth ministers for the church. Shelley began to explain some of what she and her family had been through. The hurricanes destroyed their apartment, wrecked their van and left them with little. She explained how they were incredibly frustrated with the FEMA process, had appealed for aid, and yet were refused.

When she said all this, it was as if time stopped. It was as if I looked to the side and looked towards God and said, "This is it, isn't it? This is what you sent me down here for, isn't it?" It was as if I could feel God smiling broadly at it. I knew this was it. This is the person whom "good" was due.

The service was wonderful. The island was about to re-enter hurricane season, and the pastor laid out all of the things the church had been through. It was a powerful service and sermon, but the entire time I couldn't help but wonder what I could do and who I could talk to in order to help the Claeys get the aid they deserved. There was one major problem. I had no idea what kind of aid, what good, they were actually due.

Over the next few days I began to research the various points of contact within FEMA. Trying to understand the processes that people had to go through to get aid. What was it they were missing? I wasn't looking for them to get something they weren't due; but, they were missionaries and much of what they had was destroyed. I couldn't help but think that among all the people who deserved help, they were it. Right?

So as I sorted through the various managers of the processes, I was introduced to one of the case workers. She had a big sign on her desk that read – "Queen of Awesome". She certainly was! Her smile and attitude were infectious. She had reviewed their case and found there was some information missing.

In my heart of hearts, I just knew this was going to work out. I thought, they will get the information, they will get a check, maybe even give some of it to a project that the Church needs, and so many people will be blessed. It was perfect! It had God's fingerprints all over it.

So the following Sunday I came back to the church and asked the Claeys if they minded if I tried to engage in their case. Up to this point, I had been acting on the outside; but to do more, I really felt like I needed their permission.

A few days later I had a conversation with Dave Claey, and he recounted parts of their story to me. He explained that they had been able to get out of the area before the storm hit and were in Florida when the storms came through. Much of the difficulty they encountered was trying to engage the process remotely through the chaos of a natural disaster. To add to that, the byzantine process that they had to follow required multiple submissions, some of which got lost. Each of those submissions was expensive given that they needed photos and records, all of which they were physically separated from.

In the end, he just confessed to me that he had just given up. The process was just so complex and on top of that, it was expensive. He asked me what I thought. Should he try again? I told him my story. I told him what I thought I was there to do and why God had sent me to the island.

So he agreed to try again. Over the next couple of weeks, with the help of my new friend, the Queen of Awesome, we got the package put together. The people from FEMA were happy to help and ecstatic to get it right. They were great!

A few days later I got a message to come back and see the case manager. She wanted to talk to me through what they had found. I dropped what I was doing and nearly ran over a few people as I came back. She then told me they qualified for... a low interest loan.

What? A low interest loan? That's it?!? I was stunned. It had to be a mistake. I was sure they would be eligible for a grant. As patiently as I could, I asked them to take me through the data and they did, explaining they had been through it several times themselves. Based upon the data they gave, this loan is what they qualified for.

I called Dave and Shelley and explained to them the results of what the case workers found. They were excited to hear it and said they would take a look into it. They were very thankful.

A few days later, near the end of the day, Dave called and explained that he and his family felt so much better about the process. He believed they had gotten a fair shake, but decided as a family not to take the loan. Instead they would budget and get back to where they needed to be on their own instead of using a loan.

I was honestly crushed. Not by them but by the results of the process. As I was driving back to my hotel from a very long day of work I had such frustration and anger in my heart. Why didn't this work God?!?! Why??? I explained to God how it was so perfect. They were a deserving family. I reminded Him that they were doing His work. Why not them?

(As an aside, it makes me shake my head that I had the audacity at the time to "remind" God of anything. But we will get to patience in a bit...)

The crescendo of this rage was when I explained to God, amidst all of my pleading, and whining, that all I had done is helped to restore a part of their peace.

Then it happened. A small voice inside of me, audible only in my head, asked me a very simple question. "And that wasn't enough?"

I saw it then. I remember bursting into tears at it. Of course, peace was enough.

> **Isaiah 9:6** – "For to us a child is born, to us a son is given, and the government will be on His shoulders. And He will be called Wonderful Counselor, Mighty God, Everlasting Father, *Prince of Peace*." *(Emphasis added).*

How important is God's peace? So important that he sent me 1,881 miles from Elizabethtown, KY to St. Croix, U.S. Virgin Islands to help restore a bit of that families peace. It was that important to Him. Our peace is the basis and foundation from which we operate.

To be clear, I don't want to give you the wrong impression about the Claeys. It isn't as if they were a family teetering on the edge of despair. They were and are a wonderfully strong family with a deep and abiding faith in Christ. That said, one thing I do know as an engineer is that the greatest weights require the strongest of foundations.

The Claeys, as youth ministers, are helping to raise a generation of world changers who I believe will help to transform their community, their island, and our world. That monumental task requires a strong and deep foundation if you are going to do it with excellence. A small crack in that foundation weakens the whole. To address that doubt, no matter how small in the grand scheme, means that the crack never gets the chance to get bigger. The peace that God helped to restore in this moment is important because of the crisis that never occurred because of a weakened foundation.

Sometimes foundations are taken for granted. They are out of sight, out of mind. They aren't a problem until they are. Then they REALLY are! Everything we rely on is shaken when the foundations aren't right. So they deserve our attention and careful thought. Our peace is the basis from which our strength is projected. Another way to think of it might be a dislocated shoulder. You can still use it after it is put back into place, but until it is healed you have significantly less strength. Have compromised peace in your life means you can only project so much strength into everything you do.

When we consider this foundation of peace, the first thing to remember is that God calls us to take action - to use the gifts that He has given to us.

Ephesians 6: 13 – "Therefore put on the full armor of God, so that when the day of evil comes, you may be able to stand your ground, and *after you have done everything*, to stand." *(Emphasis added)*.

"After we have done everything" speaks to our capabilities and gifts. We have been given work to do and the skills and abilities to be able to achieve what God has called us to do without special intervention from Him. Sometimes God removes an obstacle; sometimes He puts a hammer in our hand.

When we work at a job, provide a home, raise up our kids, and give them an education, they are all gifts from God. As our part in those things we extend effort in His power, for His glory and He blesses.

Past that, there is an entire class of issues and problems that are well above us. The salvation of our family and friends, healing of the sick, the wisdom that we and our leaders desperately need are all examples of things that, if we let them, can rob us of our peace.

Hebrews 12 commends us to "cast off everything that hinders". Some of what hinders is weight that we are simply never meant to carry. Instead, that weight is meant to be carried by God.

> **Philippians 4:6-7** – "Do not be anxious about anything, but in every situation, by prayer and petition, with thanksgiving, present your requests to God. And the peace of God, which transcends all understanding, will guard your heats and your minds in Christ Jesus."

In this case the mix of faith and prayer that Paul is talking about boils down to trusting in the character of God, who loves you more than you can imagine.

Prayer is relational. It is an on-going conversation with the One who made you and loves you. In 1 Thessalonians 5:17, Paul commends us to "pray without ceasing". Remember that praying without ceasing doesn't mean talking without ceasing. God gave us two ears and one mouth for a reason. It is a ratio worth remembering when we think about how much we should be listening to God versus how much we should be speaking to Him. Like so many good things in this world, to include peace, the foundation is a strong relationship with God.

So many things in this world are there to distract us from that relationship, steal our peace, and weaken the foundation of our lives. What we allow ourselves to focus on and think about has a lot to do with the peace that we carry.

> **Philippians 4:8-9** – "Finally, brothers and sisters, whatever is true, whatever is noble, whatever is right, whatever is pure, whatever is lovely, whatever is admirable—if anything is excellent or praiseworthy—think about such things. Whatever you have learned or received or heard from me, or seen in me—put it into practice. And the God of peace will be with you."

Our focus is our choice. It is the choice to feed what will give us peace, or feed what will stir up anger and discord in our lives. The choice to starve those things out that make us angry, worried, or stressed is one we have to make every single day. In the same way, we can make choices that may feel good in the moment, but ultimately they end up starving the things that bring us peace and joy. You simply cannot dip your toe into a pool and not expect it to create waves which have an effect somewhere in your life.

When you feel peace slipping away from you it is worth asking the question why? There is often a relationship between what is taking away your peace and what you expected to give you peace in the first place. As an example, if you find your peace being shaken after looking at the evening news or your bank account, it is worth asking whether those things were worthy of your trust in the first place. Jesus is the only person worthy of that kind of trust. His peace is never taken away from us, but rather it is our choice to place that trust in something inferior that puts us in a position to be worried or have anxiety.

The great news is that we can make the choice to focus and trust the right things in our lives, and by doing so we will reap a harvest of peace. The question comes down to whether or not you trust Him enough in the moment to guide your choices. It is a question of trust and focus, it is a question of faith.

Just remember that any worry we have can find a trusted resting place in His capable hands. Then that peace, which transcends all understanding, becomes the stable base from which you start every day of your life. Peace enables us to move forward in uncertainty.

He is capable. Capable of solving every problem that is beyond our reach. He loves us more than we can imagine. He knows us, our capabilities and resources. He even knows our limitations and what is beyond us.

He can be trusted with it all. He is peace.

For Further Reflection...

1. What are the things in your life that are stealing your peace?

2. How essential are those things to your life?

3. Can you change your relationship with them to transform their impact on your lives?

4. Is Biblical peace defined by what is absent or present?

5. Why is it so hard to control what we focus on in modern life?

6. What is the difference between healthy planning / preparation and worry?

7. Why is thankfulness in our prayers a necessary step in gaining peace from God?

8. What keeps you from being thankful?

The peace that we carry is the stable base from which we do everything we have been called to do. It is formed out of trust in God and the person that He is. There is nothing that you care about in this world that He didn't care about first, and more deeply.

Part of that trust in the character of God is also wrapped up in the timing and processes that God chooses to use. That trust can be elusive and many times means we need...

CHAPTER 5

Patience

But if we hope for what we do not yet have, we wait for it patiently.

Romans 8:25

ARLY IN MY ADULT LIFE I WAS AFFLICTED BY THE "RELIGIOUS SPIRIT" when it came to washing my car. Many men go through this, so I know I am not alone. I tried to always keep my cars cleaned out, shiny and generally looking sharp. There's nothing wrong with that, of course, until it becomes an obsession. During this time in my life just about every weekend you could find me washing one or both of my cars. Some of my other neighbors shook their heads, while others would give me that corny line about "being next." It wasn't every weekend, I didn't have a problem, I could quit any time I wanted to, but then again at that time I didn't want to.

It didn't help that at the time my next door neighbor was a Drill Sergeant on Fort Knox. He was a great guy who I sincerely enjoyed being around. Since we lived off the base, when we got into our neighborhood we both took our hats off, so to speak, and just became neighbors. We could share common complaints and perspectives and just relax. He and his wife were kind to us, and we to them. Just good solid neighbors. The one complaint I had with them was that his cars were always cleaner and shinier than mine were. I grumbled things about him not having any kids and such; but in the end, it was just one more reason why I was out one Saturday morning washing my wife's car.

I was out that morning cleaning the inside, getting the hose out and generally starting the process of washing the car. My son, who was about five at the time, came out and asked me what I was doing. I told him, as all good father's do, that I was washing the car and why it was important on the cosmic scale. Nations would fall if we didn't keep our cars clean. In the midst of this discussion, my hand "slipped" somehow and my son got sprayed with some of the water. At least that's how I'll tell the story. Later, as I was starting to wash the car and set the hose down, my son "tripped" over the hose and it accidently sprayed me. At least that's how he'll tell you the story. Good times, maybe even the best of times.

That is, until the fateful moment when my son asked me if he could help with the washing. I told him to go inside the house and find a sponge. He ran off. A few minutes later, as I was on the far side of the car, I saw that he had returned. It looked from my view like he was washing the car, moving from the rear door up towards the front of the car. There was one strange thing though, there was an odd sound coming from his side as he worked. I put down my sponge and walked around to his side of the car.

That's when I saw it. When he went in to get a sponge to help clean the car with, he couldn't find one. With no sponge in sight, he started to search for something in his mind that would help. What was his choice? A nail file from his Mom's purse. He was working down the side of the car, already down two doors and was about half way onto the front quarter panel.

"GAVIN!" was all I could get out. The look on my face told him everything he needed to know. He instantly dropped the nail file and looked at me in horror. "GO INSIDE!" was the only other thing I could get out. He ran!

I looked at the car and ran my fingers down the scratch. It was all the way down to the metal. I just rubbed my face and shook my head and screamed. I had to sit down on the front steps. I was sick. It was going to cost us a fair amount of money to get that fixed and it was a scar on that beautiful car.

A few moments later he came out to me on the front porch crying, telling me how sorry he was. I forgave him, but I did learn one important thing that day. I learned that if I was going to get effective help from him I was going to have to be there alongside him. I was going to have to help and guide him along the way. I learned it would be a process which would require great patience.

I'm sure we all have a story like that, either as the parent or as the child. Everyone has moments in our lives where we need to give patience, or where we need it desperately. We tend to remember the times where we have given patience, and tend to forget the moments where we need it from others.

That moment with my son is vivid in my mind. It is funny, but there are so many details of that morning I can remember. I guess that emotional moments are like that.

I fast forward a number of years to another emotional day in my son's life; the day we dropped him off to college. We had been working the entire summer searching for all of the things he would need - new bedding, things to hang on his wall, a microwave, etc. It felt like we were putting his entire life into our two cars. (In hindsight that was a bit overblown, there was still PLENTY of his stuff around the house.)

We drove the two cars, Gavin in the car with his Mom, while I traveled solo in the trail vehicle. The hour and a half trip from Elizabethtown to Lexington (Kentucky) was more than a trip down the highway to Transylvania University, it was a trip down memory lane.

As an aside, I have to say that up until this point, I had never completely understood one of the phrases in the Bible – The great and terrible day of the Lord (Joel 2:31). How could a day be great and terrible all at the same time?

Was it terribly great or greatly terrible? I didn't get it, until the day I dropped my son off.

I wanted this next step for him. He had studied hard, worked diligently, and played his heart out on the basketball court. His reward was being able to go to a wonderful university and play college basketball. I was so happy for him. What a great day in both his and our lives. Healthy birds fly, as one of my dear friends likes to say.

As I was driving down the highway, I began to play through so many other moments of my son's life. Moments of triumph. Moments of sadness. Moments of anger and frustration. Moments of joy. There were times along the way where he got it right, moments when he got it wrong. In many ways, it is the story of us all.

I began to treasure in my heart all of those moments - even the ones along the way that weren't so good. One moment like that, which was during a particularly frustrating period of high school basketball, was when my son was venting his frustrations to me in the bathroom he used. He very roughly and strongly hung his towel back onto the wall hook. The action ripped the wall hook and a good piece of the drywall clean away. The look on his face was priceless. Well, that didn't help. He learned a really valuable lesson that day, which was that acting out in your frustration never leads to anything good. (It's a lesson I've had to relearn a time or two myself.)

The process to patch the drywall and paint the area took weeks for him to get right. Could I have gotten it done in a weekend? Sure, but that wasn't the right thing to do given the circumstances. To me, there was the consequence of the action that needed to be addressed, and honestly I also thought it wasn't a bad life skill to have as well. I'm personally known as a bit of a bull in a china shop kind of person, so I have had many occasions to fix drywall in my life. I know he will need this skill eventually. The apple doesn't fall far from the tree.

The patience in that, and many other moments, helped build my son into the person he is today. Patience implies value and worth. Patience implies potential. Patience is the space where transformation happens.

There is a person I know my son can be. Every day he takes a step down the path to become that person. Is it happening as fast as I would maybe like it? No, but that is where patience comes in. Patience sees value in someone or something and is willing to wait for the process to work itself out to see it. I could say the same thing when I look at the man I see in the mirror every morning.

That day I knew I wasn't going to have him at home as much. That I wouldn't see him anywhere as much as I wanted. There was a sense of "less" that was just driving a knife into me. The combination of the feelings was so odd. It was a great and terrible day all at once.

I am convinced that moment wouldn't have been possible without patience. In some ways, having patience with my son was difficult in moments, but overall I would say it was easy because I saw and continue to see the enormous potential that he has. I love him so much and am so very proud of him. However even that statement has its own problems, because I am obviously biased towards my son, as many parents are to their kids.

That leads us to a great question. Can any of us accurately sense the potential of another? Can you even sense your own potential accurately?

Take Gideon as an example. He was a man who was a great general, great leader, and great judge for the Jewish people (see Judges 6-8). God saw the potential that he had, but that certainly wasn't how Gideon saw it at first.

> **Judges 6:15** – "'Pardon me, my lord,' Gideon replied, 'but how can I save Israel? My clan is the weakest in Manasseh, and I am the least in my family.'"

It's worth asking the question about what God saw that Gideon didn't? Is God like some heavenly pro scout who sees a tremendous upside to us that others missed? Did He look at Gideon and realize that if he just had a good diet and did CrossFit for a few months that he would develop into a great general? The next statement gives us a clue to what is really important.

> **Judges 6:16** – "The Lord answered, 'I will be with you, and you will strike down all the Midianites, leaving none alive.'"

The greatness of Gideon wasn't necessarily based upon anything about him. His greatness was to be based upon God's continued presence in his life. Without God, the incredible things that Gideon accomplished wouldn't have been possible.

My initial impression of Gideon leads me to the conclusion that he wouldn't have been my first choice for these missions. He was a guy with low self-esteem, many doubts and a poor attitude. So the question I have to ask myself, if I would have gotten it wrong with Gideon, who else am I judging incorrectly on their potential and value? Who am I not showing the right kind of patience towards because I don't see those things correctly?

Another example is Saul of Tarsus. This is how he described himself later on in his life.

> **Philippians 3:4-6** – "If someone else thinks they have reasons to put confidence in the flesh, I have more; circumcised on the eighth day, of the people of Israel, of the tribe of Benjamin, a Hebrew of Hebrews, in regard to the law, a Pharisee; as for zeal, persecuting the church; as for righteousness based on the law, faultless."

Now that's my guy! He's got the right pedigree, the right education, the right connections, and the guy always does what is right, except for that little part about persecuting the church. In this case, all of the indicators for potential were leading us in the wrong direction. This guy truly was a Christian hunter, and he was good at it. I think I might have gotten that one wrong.

It is only after a transformative encounter with God on the road to Damascus that Saul become transformed, and his purpose truly revealed. He gets a new name (Paul), a new purpose and a chance at a new legacy. It's also instructive to note that for a man who understood the Jewish people as well as he did, God chose him to go to the Gentiles (non-Jewish people) to preach the Good News. I would have gotten that wrong as well. Even with the best of intentions our sense of potential can be contrary to the plans of God.

Before the road to Damascus encounter I doubt Paul would have accurately judged his own direction, let alone his potential. He probably would have wildly misjudged it, just as I probably would have.

Each of us is "fearfully and wonderfully made" (Psalm 139:14) and because of that each of us has God given potential, and are deserving of patience as we walk towards that potential. We don't see it in others, and we often don't see it in ourselves. I have had many people in my life - parents, teachers, mentors, and coaches - who believed in me before I believed in me. That kind of belief, proved practically in patience, was transformative. It pointed me to who I could become. I'm still on that road.

God has been so patient with me in my life. I am confident to say that there isn't a day that goes by that God doesn't exercise some level of patience with me, if for no other reason than I am not the man who He knows I can become. It is out of the overflow of patience that He has given me that leads me to a place where I can be patient with others around me.

As we travel towards our potential and the potential of others, we find that humility is a necessary partner to patience.

Ecclesiastes 7:8 – "The end of a matter is better than its beginning; and patience is better than pride."

God is the only one who knows our hearts and our potential. We should place our decisions about another person's potential in His hands.

> **1 Corinthians 1:26-27** – "Brothers and sisters, think of what you were when you were called. Not many of you were wise by human standards; not many of you were influential; not many were of noble birth. But God chose the foolish things of the world to shame the wise; God chose the weak things of the world to shame the strong."

God can use who He chooses, when He chooses, and for what He chooses. That isn't up to us. Sometimes people are chosen for their purpose early in their lives, sometimes it isn't until later that they are chosen. We aren't called to discern value, we have no right to do that. The only one who has that right is the one who paid a price for us, and that is Jesus. He has called us instead to have patience with his people.

> **Colossians 3:12-13** – "Therefore, as God's chosen people, holy and dearly loved, clothe yourselves with compassion, kindness, gentleness, and patience. Bear with each other and forgive one another if any of you has a grievance against someone. Forgive as the Lord forgave you."

The Church at Colossae had Jews and Gentiles who had significant differences in their backgrounds. The Gentiles worshiped many god's that were a blend of many cultural influences. The Jewish people had God, the Old Covenant Law, and a rich cultural legacy. God had patience for them all.

There was tension at the time within the leadership of the church on how to treat the new Gentile believers. There was a common belief that the new Gentiles needed to adhere to all the tenants of the Law as well as profess faith in Christ to be saved.[5]

If we can muster any patience at all, we generally have it for those who look like us, think like us, or have the same general beliefs. God calls us to a higher standard though. Each of us comes to Christ from a different place. As we get closer to Him, we get closer to each other.

Bringing people together during that time must have taken a great deal of patience. To a new believer it must have been confusing to try and understand the relationship between the salvation that Jesus offers through the finished work on the cross versus upholding The Law, which was given to the people for their benefit and blessing. Which is it?

To a degree that tension still exists today and will until the day Christ returns. In growing, healthy churches, you will find a mixture of new and mature Christians. Patience will be required for both groups.

For those who already have made the decision to follow Jesus, there is a temptation to put a kind of moral credit score on the door of the church. You might have to look a certain way to be welcomed. You might have to have a certain level of success in your life. Maybe you have to be free from some particular sin. People often forget that there wasn't a requirement for them to come, just faith enough to accept Jesus as their savior. The Christian walk starts there for everyone.

Imagine a situation where a sick person was turned away from a hospital because they were too sick. Imagine a doctor saying come back when you are better. The whole reason you go to a hospital is to get better. To follow the analogy, to expect the patient to be cured the moment they step into the hospital is also unrealistic, but that is where the process can start, and patience can water the seeds of righteousness that are sown.

This also doesn't mean that just because you are a patient, you are qualified to be the doctor. There are responsibilities that work the other way as well. The new believer must be willing to submit to the process of transformation, realizing that it may take time to heal. It also doesn't change the truth. The patient doesn't get to determine the process; the doctor does. Perhaps that's why they are called patients in the first place. Patience is called for on all sides in the process, especially when relapses happen. Being correct in a situation never gives you the right to not be patient. It calls you to greater patience.

To continue the hospital analogy, the place where the doctor and patient start is to imagine what life would be like when the patient is fully restored. Then a plan is developed on how to get there. Boundaries, compassion, wisdom and patience are vital to the process. If we don't start with the vision of what full restoration looks like then we can miss out on the patience required to get there.

As a healthy church body, that patience is absolutely vital to unity. The Church isn't the exception to the rule where no one is ever offended or upset with differences. As we said before, that is uniformity, and that is very different than unity. We are all coming to a deeper understanding of Jesus and what faith looks like practically. When you see people of faith from various social, ethnic and economic backgrounds who wouldn't associate with each other for any other reason, you can be sure that God and patience are present. Patience can be thought of as a God given salve that settles down the irritation between us.

Many plans and schemes from the enemy work against that unity. Social media, as an example, can be an impressive tool of the enemy if used incorrectly. It is often used to separate and divide. In 2012 a study was published by Jonah Berger and Katherine Milkman about what makes online content viral.[6] Various emotional factors were considered, and would you care to guess at what topped the list? Anger. It turns out that articles that make us angry are almost three times more likely to be shared than articles that make us feel positive. That anger, distilled to its purest form, is almost universally intended to separate people into "us" and "them" categories. At this point in my life, I am convinced the most addictive thing in the world isn't a substance, but rather the feeling that comes from being right. We all crave that feeling.

Social media, by design, does that. Guided by our choices it surrounds us with similar views and opinions that highlight just how right we are. In the end it feeds something deep inside of us that probably shouldn't be nourished. It highlights how wrong they are, and how right we are. It generally makes enemies of people who we are called to love and yes, be patient with.

The apostles were a group of zealots, doctors, tax collectors, and fishermen, just to name a few. They couldn't have been more different. The marvel of that group made people wonder about what was possible with God. There is no doubt in my mind that without Jesus, who is the very embodiment of patience, that wouldn't have been possible.

The people around you are worth your patience. No matter what their views, lifestyle or background, they are. They have worth and potential you can't see and even begin to fathom. Their presence teaches us something about each other and God.

Patience is required for the sake of potential and for the sake of unity. Patience is required because God has been patient with us.

For Further Reflection...

1. What does patience imply?

2. What is the danger in trying to judge another person's value or potential?

3. Who has the ability to judge our potential?

4. What is the moral credit score required to attend your church? Should there be such a thing?

5. Do we all share the same Christian walk?

6. Why is patience so critical to unity for the Church?

7. What are practical things we can do to show patience to others?

8. How do you balance patience, love, and healthy boundaries?

9. Is patience stolen from us or do we chose not to use it?

Patience is vital to the unity of the Church. With it we will eventually see the true purpose and potential of each other developed and realized in our communities.

Patience implies value, often that we cannot see in ourselves and others. To unlock that potential to its fullest, something else is needed. Something that can usher Jesus into our lives in a powerful way. It's as if we need...

CHAPTER 6

Kindness

*Be kind and compassionate to one another, forgiving each
other, just as Christ forgave you.*

Ephesians 4:32

IN SEPTEMBER OF 2017, HURRICANE IRMA PASSED JUST NORTH OF
Puerto Rico as a Category 4. It caused widespread flooding and damage
across the island. Much as I mentioned in Chapter 4, in an amazingly unfor-
tunate series of events, a few weeks later the island was hit by Hurricane Maria
which landed as a direct hit, Category 5. At one point Maria had winds that
were sustained at 175 miles per hour. To say that the devastation to the island
was enormous is an epic understatement.

One of the experiences that put the force of the hurricane into perspective was a visit I had to the El Yunque National Forest on the eastern side of
the island. There is a valley within it that funneled and magnified the winds
to the point that it literally stripped the bark off of trees. It boggles the mind.
I didn't think something like that was even possible.

Giant power transmission towers were lying in crumpled heaps all over the island. Conductor wire from the broken power grid were strewn everywhere. The lush, green island had been stripped down and ravaged.

My wife was the choir director at North Hardin High School at the time and a good number of her students were either from Puerto Rico or were only one generation removed from the island. Teachers carry the emotional impact of their students and I can remember quite clearly her coming home and talking through tears about how upset many of her students were. They had no idea whether the loved ones they had on the island were safe or even alive. Nearly all of the communications with the island were lost. We often times fill in the gaps of our knowledge with our worst fears. This was no exception.

At my church, I pray with a wonderful husband and wife team, Jeff and Vanessa Swisher. Vanessa is originally from Puerto Rico. She had many of the same concerns for her family and loved ones. When she finally did get in contact with her family, she was very relieved to hear they were safe, but the destruction of the island weighed heavily on her heart. One morning, through tears, she described the devastation and loss to the land she grew up in.

It put a portion of the Book of Nehemiah into clear perspective. Early in the text Nehemiah is informed of the terrible living conditions of the people who lived in Jerusalem. It profoundly shakes him and he struggles with the ruined state of his ancestral home. The anguish was so clear in his demeanor and posture that King Antaxerxes asks Nehemiah what was troubling him?

Nehemiah 2:2-3 – "So the King asked me, 'Why does your face look so sad when you are not ill? This can be nothing but sadness of heart.' I was very much afraid, but I said to the King, 'May the King live forever! Why should my face not look sad when the city where my ancestors are buried lies in ruins, and its gates have been destroyed by fire?'"

The news was horrific coming out of the island and the images were shocking. It was a heavy weight that anyone related to the island carried.

At the time, I was working for the U.S. Army Corps of Engineers in the Construction Division. I got a call from my leadership asking me to be part of the team that was to go to Puerto Rico to help rebuild the power grid and by extension, return life to the island. I came home and asked my wife what she thought. The experiences with her kids made the answer easy. She told me to go and help. When you see suffering in the world, we ultimately have two choices. We can look away, or we can step in. We made the choice that day for me to step in.

I arrived to Puerto Rico in mid-October to a chaotic scene in San Juan, the capital of Puerto Rico. There were collapsed buildings and poles. Wires were down, streets washed away, and portions of the island cut off and only reachable by helicopter. At the time, it took about four and a half hours to drive from our offices in Fajardo on the east side of the island to our offices in Aguadilla on the west side of the island. In between there were three functioning traffic lights. It was madness.

The team I was blessed to work with in Task Force Power were some of the best people with whom I have ever worked. The urgency of the mission brought out the best in many of the people who worked there. It was inspiring. People from all over the world came to help. Our Corps of Engineers team that was spread all over the island came from virtually every corner of the country and beyond. (Our Office of Counsel representative actually came from duty in Korea.)

Our contractors were very much the same. It was inspiring to see so many people from so many different places come to help. On Saturdays you could easily tell where people were from, highlighted by the ball caps they wore that represented the college football team they cheered for. On some level, I expected Florida Gators, LSU Tigers and Georgia Bulldogs, but we also saw

USC Trojans, Syracuse Orangeman, Texas Longhorns, Nebraska Cornhuskers, and many others. All were there to fight the "monster" in front of us.

Among the many challenges we had, material was the greatest. Our initial estimates were that we had 60,000 power poles, 17,000,000 feet of conductor cable, and maybe as many as 250,000 fuses to replace. The initial estimates were close to $6 billion dollars in damages to the power grid alone. When we estimated what we would look like, government and contractor team together at full strength, we estimated our burn rate to be around $40 million a day.

The material challenge was exacerbated by the terrible disaster season the United States had already endured. Hurricane's Harvey, Irma, Maria, and Nate had already had an effect on the nation. Significant wildfires in Washington, Oregon and California further strained the materials available to us. The materials that we needed simply didn't exist. It had to be manufactured and then sent to us.

On top of that, you can never forget that Puerto Rico is an island, and everything had to be shipped there. Barges could only give us so much space for restoration materials because they still had to still bring in the everyday materials that were necessary to sustain the island. At one point we were even chartering giant Antonov aircraft at $225,000 per flight to bring in equipment and supplies. The undertaking was massive!

All of this lead to frustratingly slow progress. The men and women who we worked with became geniuses in taking downed material and repurposing it to bring up parts of the power grid. Anything we could do to scratch and claw for progress was done. Days turned into weeks, and weeks turned into months. The progress was there, but it just wasn't enough.

That leads me to Christmas Eve morning. It was shaping up to be a really bad day. Our team was tired and mentally exhausted. I credit some exceptional leadership by Colonel John Lloyd, Deputy Chief Linda Murphy, and Chief of Operations Phil Tilly with keeping the team together and moving forward despite extremely challenging conditions. It was not easy by any measure, yet they kept us together.

Even so, we were desperately missing our families back home. Many of us had missed Thanksgiving with them and now we were separated again for Christmas. On top of that we knew that there were families all over the island that were going to wake up Christmas morning with no power in their homes. There was a gut level rage that most of us carried about how unacceptable we found the situation to be. I know as a Christian I should (and do) care about all people, but there was something particularly galling about this happening in my country. This island is part of the United States, and this kind of misery should never last this long. We were doing everything we could, but we just knew it wasn't enough.

I reported to work that morning in a foul mood. I just wanted to be alone and miserable. Instead, my friend Phil Tilly tapped me on the shoulder and told me that he was going across the street to a Mass service and that I should come. I remembered looking at him for a long moment, throwing my pen down and saying, "Let's go."

Phil Tilly had also convinced one of the Army captains serving with us to go and the group of us began to walk from the Puerto Rican Electric Power Authority (PREPA) headquarters where our offices were down the street to a tiny Parish called Parroquia La Monserrate. I'm not a practicing Catholic, but one thing I know, if I know anything, is that I am welcome in the House of God.

To say that we stood out like a sore thumb might still be understating it. Phil and I were wearing a very distinctive white polo shirt that identified us as members of the team there to work on the power grid. The captain stood out even more in his military camouflage uniform. I really wasn't sure what to expect, or what kind of a welcome we would receive.

When we entered the parish the people there greeted us in Spanish. They were so welcoming, even though we had absolutely no idea what each of us were saying. I know just enough Spanish to order from a menu and find a bathroom but that was about the extent of it. Eventually one woman was brought to us who knew how to speak English. She brought the priest to us and they welcomed us warmly.

As the church filled, we began to settle in. The service started and there was something special there. I grew up in a Lutheran Church, so I am no foreigner to liturgy, but many times when I have visited churches that practice that, it is dead. There is no life in it. This was not the case here. Not at all.

As the service progressed, even though my Spanish was extremely limited, I recognized The Lord's Prayer, the Apostle's Creed and some of the hymns that were being sung. The environment washed over us, and I could feel something being lifted from us. There was such joy there.

I even remember looking up to see the Priest whispering something to the two acolytes who were sitting to his side and the two of them having to cover their mouths to keep them from laughing out loud. Their smiles were contagious as was their spirit.

In a Catholic Mass, there is a certain cadence and rhythm to it and, for better or worse, very little is ever allowed to interrupt it. That is what made the next part so curious to us.

What I interpreted as the Priests final closing prayer was halted and the cadence was broken. The three of us looked up from the prayer to see what the Priest was saying, and as he spoke, the entire congregation turned, looked at us and smiled. My heart honestly skipped a beat.

When he finished he pointed to the woman who had spoken to us. She looked us in the eyes and said, "On behalf of our church we would like to thank our guests for coming today and for coming to our island to help restore power and light to our homes. May God bless you and your families." Tears began to stream down our faces as the church broke into a round of applause for us. It is an act of kindness that I will never forget.

And we thought we came there to bless them.

That moment completely transformed the day and how I saw it. It is as close as I have ever come to being able to understand the verse in Acts 9 where it talks about "something like scales fell from Saul's eyes, and he could see again." The church, the people, and even the decorations were brighter. The smiles were more joyful and my heart truly lighter.

After work that night, I walked the streets of Old San Juan. There is an area of the city where they have a giant walkway that is covered in Christmas lights. I remembered tears coming to my eyes and thinking that I hadn't seen anything so beautiful in a long, long time. Everything had been transformed and been made new, even in the midst of the work we still had to accomplish.

It was so strange. For someone who grew up in the mid-west, Christmas is a wonderful season, but it is cold, dark and dreary if not for the Christmas lights. (I think that's why I tend to put up so many.) This was completely different. The warm tropical weather brings everyone out in a celebration that is something to behold. At the end of the day, I knew that God had been revealed to me in a new way, and it was ushered in with kindness.

It got me thinking about that Christmas and the kindness I was shown. I thought about Joseph, the man who would be responsible to act as Jesus's earthly father, and one of his decisions stood out.

> **Matthew 1:19** – "Because Joseph her husband was faithful to the law, and yet did not want to expose her to public disgrace, he had a mind to divorce her quietly."

At this point all Joseph knows is that the woman he was supposed to marry was pregnant, and it wasn't by him. If you place yourself into that narrative, I am sure you would agree that thinking of Mary's well-being would probably not be at the forefront of your mind. There would be an enormous amount of hurt and emotion to work through, and yet within that I would describe his actions, simply and amazingly, as kind.

When God looked over all of the Earth for the man and the woman who would raise His son, He chose a woman of faith, and a kind man. If you are looking to raise Jesus in your home, I think you could do far worse than to emulate that as parents. Kindness ushered in Jesus then, and it continues to do so today.

> **Romans 2:4** – "Or do you show contempt for the riches of His kindness, forbearance, and patience, not realizing that God's kindness is intended to lead you to repentance?"

Kindness at the end of patience (forbearance) is transformative. The Jewish people had to wait 400 hundred years for Christ to come and at the end of that patience, kindness ushered in Jesus to our world. The extraordinary patience that the people of Puerto Rico showed in the face of the hurricanes (imagine what would happen if part of Florida were without power for two months or more) followed by their kindness brought Jesus in a new way into mine. I will be forever thankful.

There are many moments of special kindness that Jesus showed to the people who were around them, but I think the one that is most instructive is when Jesus washed the feet of His disciples.

> **John 13:1-17** – "It was just before the Passover Festival. Jesus knew that the hour had come for him to leave this world and go to the Father. Having loved His own who were in the world, He loved them to the end.

> The evening meal was in progress, and the devil had already prompted Judas, the son of Simon Iscariot, to betray Jesus. Jesus knew that the Father had put all things under His power, and that He had come from God and was returning to God; so He got up from the

meal, took off his outer clothing, and wrapped a towel around his waist. After that, he poured water into a basin and began to wash His disciples' feet, drying them with the towel that was wrapped around Him.

He came to Simon Peter, who said to Him, 'Lord, are you going to wash my feet?' Jesus replied, 'You do not realize now what I am doing, but later you will understand.' 'No,' said Peter, 'you shall never wash my feet.' Jesus answered, 'Unless I wash you, you have no part with me.'

'Then, Lord,' Simon Peter replied, 'not just my feet but my hands and my head as well!' Jesus answered, 'Those who have had a bath need only to wash their feet; their whole body is clean. And you are clean, though not every one of you.' For he knew who was going to betray him, and that was why he said not everyone was clean.

When he had finished washing their feet, he put on his clothes and returned to his place. 'Do you understand what I have done for you?' he asked them. 'You call me 'Teacher' and 'Lord,' and rightly so, for that is what I am. Now that I, your Lord and Teacher, have washed your feet, you also should wash one another's feet. I have set you an example that you should do as I have done for you. Very truly I tell you, no servant is greater than his master, nor is a messenger greater than the one who sent him. Now that you know these things, you will be blessed if you do them.'"

Jesus showed profound patience with His disciples as He walked with them during the years of His ministry. His decision to punctuate that by using some of the final moments of His life to show kindness should not be missed. That act of kindness brought something new into the lives of the disciples and transformed how they saw each other and the people they were to humbly serve.

This kindness had no strings attached. There was no ulterior motive to the kindness, other than that it would be passed along to someone else. Kindness with an expectation of return isn't kindness, it's a transaction.

This can be a great hindrance to the prayers we pray and interact with each other. Fervent prayer hopes for transformation and blessing without any expectation of return. The reward, if you can frame it in a different way, is Jesus being ushered into their lives and yours in a new way.

Prayer is one of the greatest acts of kindness imaginable when focused on another. You are asking Almighty God to act on behalf of the person you are praying for. Within that prayer is the possibility of release of His resources, healing, grace, and mercy. Those prayers may result in kindness that flows through a divine act, or perhaps it is through our hands or another. All of that without the expectation of return to ourselves.

As a contrast to that lack of expectation, think about going into a fast food restaurant and paying a meal. That doesn't result in transformation or blessing, it results in a transaction. Relationship isn't my expectation. I give something with a distinct expectation of a defined return. There is nothing wrong with that, but we cannot make the mistake that thinking that this kind of economy will result in a transformed heart and for Jesus to come into a situation in a new way.

Many people have been damaged severely by this kind of transactional kindness. That brand of kindness says - if I put in enough quarters of kindness eventually the vending machine will drop out what I desire. I've seen it in churches and in the mission field, where if a certain kind of response isn't given the kindness isn't given anymore. I've seen it in relationships and marriages where kindness is used as a subtle act of control, and if the desired outcome doesn't follow, the kindness will stop. I've met people, rich and poor alike, who view every act of kindness with suspicion because they have come to not trust the intentions of any giver. It is a profoundly sad place to see someone live. True kindness doesn't flow out of what we expect in return, it flows out of the kindness we have already been shown by God.

The good news is that real kindness can change that. An unmerited, unexpected blessing at the end of patience with no expectation of return can change hearts and lives. That act ushers in Jesus and the transformation that only He can bring to our world, our work, and our relationships. All of our prayers and actions, even for our enemies as Jesus commanded[7], should be filtered through that kindness.

Perhaps more than anything else the world needs, it is kindness and the transformation it brings.

For Further Reflection...

1. Where have you had to show the greatest patience in your life?

2. When is it easy to be kind? Are those moments transformative?

3. When is it hard to be kind? Are those moments transformative?

4. What is the danger in expecting something in return for kindness?

5. Are those moments of transactional kindness transformative?

6. Who is worth being kind to?

7. Is a certain level of morality or obedience required before we can be kind to someone?

8. What steals kindness from our hearts?

Kindness is an unmerited, unexpected blessing at the end of patience with no expectation of return. When we do that we can transform relationships in unexpected ways.

Modeling that behavior in our daily lives is powerful and essential to an effective life as a Christian. That leads us to another essential element critical to being effective. It leads us to...

CHAPTER 7

Goodness

Therefore, my dear friends, as you have always obeyed
– not only in my presence, but now much more in my
absence – continue to work out your salvation with fear
and trembling, for it is God who works in you to will and
to act in order to fulfill His good purpose.

Philippians 2:12-13

WHEN YOU LOOK UP "GOODNESS" IN THE DICTIONARY, THERE IS one explanation of the word that bears some further thought - the phrase, as an exclamation, is as a substitute for God.[8]

I think the context to which the dictionary is referring is where, in an attempt to not take the Lord's name in vain, we exclaim "goodness!" instead of "God." It's not necessarily a bad practice, but it got me thinking.

What if we saw that definition in a slightly different light?

I have a friend of mine, Annette, who is one of the kindest people you will ever meet. She sees the best in people. She can't bring herself to look away from someone in need. She is "Super Mom" to her son and his friends. She volunteers her time coaching kids in basketball. (She even put off back surgery to be able to coach them.) Her involvement doesn't stop at the end of the season; she has tutored those same kids in reading, or whatever subject they need, and encourages the kids to be as good off the court as they are on it. Is she perfect? No, and she never would claim to be, but the simple fact is that I know Jesus better because I know Annette. Each way she cares for others shows me a little bit more about how Jesus might do it, and in turn how I should care for others as well.

I have a friend of mine, Tom, who is one of the humblest men I have ever met. He is a doctor and spends his days compassionately helping to enable care for others. He is also heavily involved in the youth program for our church, and not just for the sake of his own kids. He has served his county in the Army as a doctor, serves and helps others in our city as a leader, as well as serving as an elder for our church. Even though he would never say it, he is one of the wisest, most humble men I have ever met. I love the man's heart. Is he perfect? No, and he would never claim to be, but the simple fact is that I know Jesus better because I know Tom. Each way that he humbly serves shows me a little more about how Jesus might serve others, as in turn shows me a little bit more about how I should do it as well.

I have a friend of mine, Grace, who has a heart the size of Pennsylvania, where she is from. I have the privilege of serving with her on the Mission's Committee for my church. She has a heart that cares for every single person she meets and can always be found volunteering to help with our Vacation Bible School or one of the local missions who needs help. Maybe most impactful, I will never forget seeing the way she loved her husband in his final days before he passed away. The world will tell you a hundred different selfish, shiny, and plastic ways to love, but that day I saw what was authentic. She is a remarkable person. Is she perfect? No, and she would never claim to be, but the simple fact is that I know Jesus better because I know Grace. Each way that she loves those around her shows me a little more about how Jesus might love others, even when they can give nothing in return, and in the process shows me a little more about how I should love others as well.

If you think about it, I'm sure you have friends just like this as well. I hope you have many. You might have even been lucky enough to have parents like this, or a coach, or mentor who showed you a little bit about what Jesus looks like by the way they interacted with the world. The real outcome of this fruit - goodness - is showing the world what Jesus looks like before they ever read a single thing about Him.

Humanity representing Him on Earth has been His plan from the beginning.

> **Genesis 1:26-28** – "Then God said, 'Let us make mankind in our image, in our likeness, so that they may rule over the fish in the sea and the birds in the sky, over the livestock and all the wild animals, and over all the creatures that move along the ground.' So God created mankind in His own image, in the image of God He created them; male and female he created them. God blessed them and said to them, 'Be fruitful and increase in number; fill the earth and subdue it. Rule over the fish in the sea and the birds in the sky and over every living creature that moves in the ground.'"

In the beginning God created us in His image. To phrase it in a slightly different way, He created us as image bearers to the world. Before the fall, Adam and Eve represented God in the everyday world. They were to rule over it as they completed the work that God had set out for them. The world was supposed to see God through the two He created by their perfect acts of goodness, love, wisdom or compassion.

It is important to note that they were never meant to do it without him. The wisdom to do each of those well is only unlocked through relationship with God. People will often try to reduce Christianity to a set of rules to follow when at its core the basis of Christianity is relationship.

And not to say that rules are bad, they provide us with guard rails to keep us safe, but no book could ever give you all of answers to every test you will ever face in your life. Instead God offers relationship, and through that relationship the wisdom to navigate life. So at a fundamental level our goodness, or the ability to represent God in the world around us, depends on wisdom we receive from and through Him in relationship.

So how do we practically gain the wisdom to represent God well? The great news is that all we have to do is ask.

> **James 1:5-8** – "If any of you lacks wisdom, you should ask God, who gives generously to all without finding fault, and it will be given to you. But when you ask, you must believe and not doubt, because the one who doubts is like a wave of the sea, blown and tossed by the wind. That person should not expect to receive anything from the Lord. Such a person is double-minded and unstable in all they do."

I'm thankful that God is always willing to give me wisdom. I don't have to clean up my life or achieve some level of perfection before He will give it to me. Some people think the reverse is true, but by asking God for His wisdom and then following it that is how we start to clean up our lives and look a little bit more like Jesus to those around us each day. As a contrast, it is our best thinking that gets us into the tough situations we often find ourselves in.

As for being double-minded, it is easy to understand when you put it into perspective. If you ask the very personification of wisdom for advice, and then do the opposite, what do we expect to have happen? Not much good, I can assure you.

As was such for Adam and Eve. When sin entered the world a fracture occurred that separated God and Man. No longer would man be able to claim being a perfect image bearer or reflection of the Father. Each time they sinned, they or their descendants (us) choose to reflect the image of someone different.

It would take several thousand years before another perfect example would come along. Jesus, who is described as the second Adam in 1 Corinthians 15:47-49, came back and perfectly "re-presented" God to humanity. Wherever people saw Jesus, whatever He was doing, was a perfect image of the Father.

Jesus knew what it meant to do this on a practical level.

> **John 5:19-20** – "Jesus gave them this answer: 'Very truly I tell you, the Son can do nothing by himself; he can do only what He sees his Father doing, because whatever the Father does the Son also does. For the Father loves the Son and shows him all he does. Yes, and He will show Him even greater works than these, so that you will be amazed.'"

Every movement, every action and every word that Jesus spoke was born out of the relationship He had with the Father. That type of relationship and reflection of His character is available to us today. By being fully man, as well as fully God, Jesus came to show us what life could be like. If He was only God, then I would still be impressed, but it would be a standard I could not achieve. By being fully man, Jesus shows us what is possible in our own lives; which is to be able to demonstrate the goodness and the character of God in our everyday lives - to fully and properly be an image bearer of the one who loves us.

I find it interesting to contrast the work of God, versus the work of the enemy, summed up perfectly in the Book of John.

> **John 10:10** – "The thief comes only to steal and kill and destroy; I have come that they may have life, and have it to the full."

If you want to judge any action you have taken in your life, wondering whether it was from God and His wisdom, or to put it another way, whether you represented God well in a moment, you could do much worse than to ask yourself the question of whether the decision or input you gave produced life or death. It isn't immediate or easy to see sometimes but, down at the very bottom of it, one of the two will be proven by the passage of time. Life or death. To choose to represent God well is to represent abundant life.

It seems like a tall task that we don't have the innate authority to make happen, but when we perfectly match our Father's heart then we can move through the world with His authority.

Whenever I think about this, I go back to my time as a lieutenant in the Army. I was blessed to serve under and with some amazing officers and non-commissioned officers. The first battalion sergeant major I served with was Command Sergeant Major Gainey. (He would later go on to be the first Senior Enlisted Advisor to the Chairman of the Joint Chiefs of Staff.) He was an outstanding soldier who demonstrated discipline, dedication and caring for soldiers in everything he did.

Technically, as a second and first lieutenant, I outranked Sergeant Major Gainey. Does that mean I ignored what he told me? Absolutely not. The wise junior officer never ignores the direction, wisdom or advice of the senior non-commissioned officer. Sergeant Major Gainey, probably more than any other soldier I ever served with, truly represented his commander in the field. We trusted his word and his example, as if it were from the commander himself. He was, and I would bet my last dollar, still is today – an image bearer of what a soldier and citizen should be.

We can have that same relationship with God as His "image bearer." When we listen to His voice, follow His directions, we then are able to move throughout the world and carry a measure of His power. That is the power of goodness.

> **John 15:5-8** – "I am the vine; you are the branches. If you remain in me and I in you, you will bear much fruit; apart from me you can do nothing. If you do not remain in me, you are like a branch that is thrown away and withers; such branches are picked up, thrown into the fire and burned. If you remain in me and my words remain in you, ask whatever you wish, and it will be done for you. This is to my Father's glory, that you bear much fruit, showing yourselves to be my disciples."

When we seek the Father's heart in a matter and ask for His wisdom, the strength and the power to fulfill the commands comes with it. It is through that strength that we get to represent God on earth. Through relationship with Him, others see the connection with Jesus in us and come to it themselves.

> **1 Peter 3:12-15** – "Who is going to harm you if you are eager to do good? But even if you should suffer for what is right, you are blessed. 'Do not fear their threats; do not be frightened.' But in your hearts revere Christ as Lord. Always be prepared to give an answer to everyone who asks you to give a reason for the hope that you have. But do this with gentleness and respect, keeping a clear conscience, so that those who speak maliciously against your good behavior in Christ may be ashamed of their slander."

The church was suffering persecution at the time this was written. Peter knew that if the church responded with the same kind of persecution and hate they were suffering under, their witness would be compromised. They would no longer be re-presenting God, no longer bearing His image.

Any behavior, especially a bad one, is never changed by giving the same in return. It is worth considering when you are tempted to "fight fire with fire" to remember that the fire department generally uses water. Anger won't change anger. Hate won't change hate. It is only when we meet those with God's wisdom and goodness that we can hope to change the world.

How we fight matters. How we win matters. It is only by following the wisdom of God and displaying his goodness to the world that ultimately anything is changed. The enemy does not care what cause you serve as long as you leave the character of Jesus to defend it or achieve it.

It is the goodness that we reflect that leads others to see Jesus, and that can be transformative. It isn't our political views, our scathing social media posts, or our sports team affiliation. In the end it is our relationship with Christ that feeds wisdom into us, shapes our daily decisions, and allows us to re-present God as his image bearer, showing his goodness, and this changes the world.

In the end it begs the question, who will you represent today?

For Further Reflection...

1.   What does it mean to be an image bearer?

2.   Do people know Jesus better because they know you?

3.   What does it take to represent Jesus well in our daily lives?

4.   Why do we fail to ask for wisdom as we go through our lives?

5.   What is the outcome?

6.   What does it take to move with God's authority in life?

7.   What does goodness look like?

8.   What does goodness not look like?

9.   What do you picture when you think of goodness being stolen from us? What can you do to keep that from happening?

Goodness allows us to move through the world, representing God well. People will see us and, as an extension see Jesus when we do it well.

This isn't easy and the transformative power of Goodness doesn't always happen immediately. It is almost as if we needed something else to lean on during the time we wait for goodness to yield its harvest. We need...

CHAPTER 8

Faithfulness

*He holds success in store for the upright, He is a shield to
those whose walk is blameless, for He guards the course of
the just and protects the way of His faithful ones.*

Proverbs 2:7-8

I'VE ALWAYS BEEN A CLOSET HISTORIAN. EVEN THOUGH MOST OF MY
life has been spent professionally as an engineer, I have always been fasci-
nated with history. History is full of stories of adventure and triumph. Victory
and defeat. The story of us all.

Military history holds its own fascination. I am blessed to have visited
many battlefields and spaces where some of the most important moments in
the world's history happened: Gettysburg, Verdun, and Normandy just to
name a few. Each of them are amazing places filled with incredible stories of
bravery.

The equipment used by the armies involved in those battles has a special
place in my heart. To understand the decisions that the leaders made, one has
to understand the equipment they carried and operated. It's like looking back

into a world with pay phones and then asking yourself why would they use those instead of cell phones? You can't fully understand the critical moments of history without the context of the tools and equipment.

One summer while I was stationed in Germany I had special opportunity. The battalion I was in deployed to the Combined arms Maneuver Training Center (CMTC). The name has changed since then, but essentially this space is used to train many different armies in Europe. As we were about to begin training I got notice that we were to keep certain roads clear to allow elements of the German 10th Panzer Division to come out of the field. This was a routine procedure to minimize any risk of vehicle strikes between large armored vehicles, but it provided a special opportunity.

Instead of going to dinner that evening, I was going to watch the units come out of the field. I wanted to see their equipment in motion. It would give me insights into the German Army and the way they operated. In some ways it felt like stepping back in time, while seeing the present all at once. They are our Allies but were once our foes. We also viewed them as peers. We knew their equipment was first class, that they trained hard, and were disciplined and dedicated soldiers. As an armor officer, I particularly wanted to see the Leopard 2 Tank in motion. It is very much viewed as one of the best main battle tanks in the world.

Positioned at a crossroads, a little bit before the time they were scheduled to come, I began to hear a guttural rumbling sound coming out of the hills. I knew they were coming!

The sound grew louder and louder. Yet they weren't there. There were several times I just KNEW they had to be right around the corner because it was so loud; but they still weren't there. At a certain point I thought I was going to need hearing protection (in hindsight I probably did, but I was caught up in the moment), and then they finally appeared. Tanks, personnel carriers, artillery pieces all made their way by.

I was struck by something about the differences between the United States and the German way of war. It may seem counter-intuitive, but relatively speaking the Abrams tank, which the United States uses, is a relatively quiet tank. If its engine is turned away from you, you can be only a few hundred meters from it and not be able to hear it. Our Army's idea is that in the defense the first time the enemy should know we are present is when rounds of ammunition are coming their way.

Contrasting that with the German style, they want others to know they are coming. For as long as they have had tanks, the Germans have emphasized the psychological aspects of this kind of warfare. In World War II the German Tiger and Panther tanks were terrifying. The two tanks greatly outclassed the earlier versions of the Allied Sherman Tank, with virtually no chance of being able to destroy the tank through its frontal armor. Soldiers described over and over again how their blood would run cold when they would hear the unmistakable sound of a Tiger Tank coming.

The shoulder fire bazooka the American soldiers carried would barely scratch the paint. The shells from a Sherman tank would bounce harmlessly off the front and portions of the sides of the tank. The only solid chance an Allied Tank had was to get a shot in from the rear. The despair that must have come over them when they realized nothing in their possession would assure them victory must have been terrifying.

The German way of war is to have you stew in your fear. To sow despair into your heart. To know they are coming, and there isn't anything you can do about it.

It's almost as if the sound of the German Tank engine is singing a song of despair.

You can't win.

You don't even have the tools to win.

All your efforts mean nothing.

Your leaders don't care about you.

They have been lying to you. Give up now.

Anyone feel like that from time to time? Our enemy seeks to have us surrender to our fears and give up the fight before we even start it.

> **1 Peter 5:8-9** – "Be alert and of sober mind. Your enemy the devil prowls around like a roaring lion looking for someone to devour. Resist him, standing firm in the faith, because you know that the family of believers throughout the world is undergoing the same kind of sufferings."

You marriage will never change.

You're always going to be stuck in this job.

No one will ever notice your talents.

All this work you put into doing the right thing? It's not worth it. Those people telling you to do the right thing? What do they know? They are lying to you. This isn't going to work. It hasn't before, and it never will.

Am I the only one? I know I'm not.

The enemy and society at large whispers all sorts of things in our ears. The movies, television shows and commercials we watch all sing a song of discontentment and failure into our lives. If you only had a certain car, then you would be content. If you only lost 20 pounds, or gained this much muscle, then you would finally be happy.

Romantic movies might be the worst of them all. Many of them portray emotional abuse or stalking as what is ideal. In any case what is shown is either sanitized or unrealistic. Then we wonder why things go horribly wrong when we try those things out in real relationships.

These whispers get louder and louder as the holidays approach. We feel lonely, depressed and isolated. We somehow think that unless everything is perfect, like some Norman Rockwell painting, that our holidays are a failure.

Our families are most often about as far away from those fantasy scenes as can possibly be imagined. Thanksgiving alone should be counted as a miracle for the mere fact that people of such different political views and personal backgrounds can sit at the table together for more than 30 minutes.

Sometimes the fireworks that come out of Thanksgiving dinners that I have heard about make the displays we see on the 4th of July seem tame.

Our disappointment comes from the gap between expectation and the reality we exist in. We see these times coming from a distance and the whispers start about how things will never change. About how we will never make it. We have fights in our minds with people we might never even talk to about subjects that may never come up. We imagine conversations and fill in the gaps of what we don't know with our fears.

Each of them have an element of truth, which is what makes them such effective lies. We must remember that even though what we are told may have a small piece of truth in it, it is not the <u>complete</u> truth. Faithfulness understands that there are more voices to consider than just the one the world is presenting in front of you.

> **Hebrews 11:1-3** – "Now faith is the confidence in what we hope for and assurance about what we do not see. This is what the ancient were commended for. By faith we understand that the universe was formed at God's command, so that what is seen was not made out of what was visible."

Faith is factoring God into the equation. Faith does not ignore the problems and the issues. Faith sees them for what they are; the issues, the complexities, the hurt, the pain, the history, but it does not give those things a preeminent place. Faith balances out whatever scales you may have with the belief in His goodness, His mercy, and his timing. Faithfulness is putting that faith into action.

It takes courage, and often times it takes accountability. Soldiers don't fight alone, and neither should we. Our lives, in so many ways are about fighting for the blessings that God wants to give us. It takes help. As part of our local Emmaus community (a Christian organization formed out of local churches focused on discipleship), I meet weekly with a group of men who over the years have been such great friends. They have prayed for, confronted, challenged, and loved me even when I fail. I do the same for them. None of us are perfect, far from it, but we know we are better together.

I am blessed that in every season of my life God has brought alongside a Christian brother or sister to encourage and walk through the tough moments of my life with me. That kind of combined strength emphasized the kind of community God wants for each of us.

Does this kind of accountability and counsel solve every problem we ever encounter? No, it doesn't. Anyone who tells you otherwise is selling you something, and it isn't worth buying. Jesus himself assured us that in this world we would have trouble. The fact is that some issues in our lives will not be corrected this side of heaven. Yet it is still our choice on which path will we follow. We can choose belief in the wisdom that God so freely offers to us, or to give up and take a path we perceive to be easier and less costly. It is a false choice. Sin always costs us more than we want to pay, and takes us further than we ever would want to go, and keeps us longer than we want to stay.

So how do we fight back? How do we fight faithfully?

Prayer is the first great act of faith in any situation. Prayer, when done right, acknowledges God and His wisdom in any situation. It is a two way conversation with the One who made you and loves you more than you can imagine. It takes account of His goodness and His love and realizes that there isn't any problem in this world that He doesn't have an answer for. It also believes that there isn't any problem in this world that He doesn't already know about, and care about more than you. Praying into the future for those you care about is an act of loving faith.

As a way to think about it, the Army has a phrase about using field artillery: the artillery barrage sets the conditions for a successful attack. Prayer does the same thing. In a spiritual sense, it sets the conditions for success. It is an exchange that brings wisdom and understanding. It is firing heavenly artillery forward in time into situations you care about. It gives a sense of timing and of technique that is necessary in a moment. Should you speak? Should you be silent? Should you act? Should you be still? Prayer helps to answer those questions. Wisdom in so many ways is situational.

We also need Christian community. We need people, young and old, who are pouring wisdom and the courage to be faithful into our lives.

> **Proverbs 15:22** – "Plans fail for lack of counsel, but with many advisors they succeed."

> **Proverbs 24:22** – "Surely you need guidance to wage war, and victory is won through many advisors."

Sometimes we need that counsel and resource, sometimes we are that counsel and resource, that is why community is so important. These things help us look into the face of any situation, no matter how dire, and help us to act in faith. Faithfulness has us act in the way God wants us to, even in the face of the unknown.

As we live out our lives there are four broad categories of situations that make demands of our faith. It might be that you encounter a situation you didn't see coming and, out of nowhere, your faith is tested. In Luke 1:26-38 you can see a great example with Mary, who didn't at all see it coming, as an angel appears to her and tells her she would be the mother of The Son of the

Most High. Her response in faith is so remarkable and is why we still talk about it today.

Another category might be the long term struggle where you have received some kind of promise or word from God. Whether it is by prophetic word or by prayer you might get a sense that God has promised something to you. The story of Abraham in chapters 12 – 21 of Genesis is an incredible example of this kind of faith. Abraham was 75 years old when he received a promise to make him into a great nation. That promise wouldn't be fulfilled for another 25 years with the birth of Isaac. Abraham displayed great faith in the promise by believing what God said. Long term struggles add complexity and difficulty to our faith response, but it is easier to deal with them when you have a promise to lean on, as it was in this case with Abraham.

Yet there are times when we have a faith struggle, sometimes long term, where we don't know whether things will ever change or what the outcome will be. In these cases there is no promise or word to rely upon. The story of Shadrach, Meshach, and Abednego and the furnace is a great example in Daniel 3:1-18. King Nebuchadnezzar creates a golden idol and demands everyone worship it when they hear music. The three refuse despite the very real threat to throw them into a deadly furnace. Right before they are thrown in they make one last statement of faith – "King Nebuchadnezzar, we do not need to defend ourselves before you in this matter. If we are thrown into the blazing furnace, the God we serve is able to deliver us from it, and He will deliver us from Your Majesty's hand. But even if He does not, we want you to know, Your Majesty, that we will not serve your gods or worship the image of gold you have set up." To see the consequences of your decision put right in front of you, and yet to still act in faith is amazing and an example for all time. Yes, it worked out for the three of them, but that shouldn't diminish the act of faith just because we know how it ends.

The final, and most difficult, category of demand on our faith is when you have a situation you know will not change, but God has called you to be faithful anyway. There are many examples of this in the Bible, but one that stands out to me is in Jeremiah 29:10-11. This includes one of the most quoted passages of scripture in verse 11 – ""For I know the plans I have for you", declares the Lord, "plans to prosper you and not to harm you, plans to give you a hope and a future."" That is such an encouraging verse but it demands the context of the previous verse to be understood fully. ""This is what the Lord says: "When seventy years are completed for Babylon, I will come to you and fulfill my good promise to bring you back to this place.""

Verse 10 might be a word of hope if you received it as a ten year old child. It would be very different if you were sixty. Then you know that no matter how hard you pray, you will not be coming back to your home in your lifetime. Despite that reality, many acted in faith and the Jewish people thrived and survived.

Just about every person I know who has a faith I admire has something like this in their life. Something that they don't believe will change, but they keep on being faithful anyway. It is remarkable. Where does that come from?

The answer to that begins with a simple question – will you ever change? The truth is we sin, and we fail God every day. Yes, we are walking a path towards looking more and more like Jesus every day, but as long as we are tied to our earthly flesh, we will never be perfect and we will continue to fail. On some levels at least – we will never change. What is God's response? Faithfulness. He will never leave us or forsake us.[9]

It is out of the overflow of faithfulness that God has shown to us that we to can be faithful in situations we encounter, whether we think they will ever change or we know they won't. It is a call to act in a certain way, despite the situation, and sets us apart as examples to the world around us. And what happens when we act in that faith?

Philippians 1:27-28 – "Whatever happens, conduct yourself in a manner worthy of the gospel of Christ.

> Then, whether I come and see you or only hear about you in my absence, I will know that you stand firm in the one Spirit, striving together as one for the faith of the gospel with being frightened in any way by those who oppose you. This is a sign to them that they will be destroyed, but that you will be saved – and that by God." *(Emphasis Added.)*

Did you catch that? When we are faithful, the Spirit inside of us begins to speak. It begins to sing a song of despair to the powers of Hell working against us in our lives.

You can't win.

You don't even have the tools to win.

All your efforts mean nothing.

Your leaders don't care about you.

They have been lying to you. Give up now.

We can listen to the enemy or speak into situations based upon our faithfulness to God. We can choose to let despair whisper to us, or we can choose to pray, seek the counsel of our Christian community, and then act in faith. When we do that our actions roar and echo into the deepest part of Hell that they will not have the final word. God's unending faithfulness to us demands a response.

For Further Reflection...

1. What areas of your life do you find it most difficult to act in faith?

2. Why is that?

3. What areas of community do you already have in your life?

4. What effect has their wisdom had on your actions, good or bad?

5. Does faith always solve the problem?

6. Why should we choose faith?

7. What areas of your life do you need counsel in? Where can you go to find that counsel?

8. What steals our faith? Is it easier to steal in good times or bad?

Faithfulness is the ability to stand in any situation and act in a way that honors God and takes into account His wisdom, goodness and mercy. Faithfulness allows us to broadcast to the world the hope we carry in Jesus. That despite what we see in front of us, we will do what is right.

This is far from easy though. For us to be able to look into the eyes of desperate situations (especially when it concerns things or people we are passionate about) takes an amazing amount of strength. It takes courage, it take wisdom, it takes...

CHAPTER 9

Gentleness

*And the Lord's servant must not be quarrelsome but
must be kind to everyone, able to teach, not resentful.
Opponents must be gently instructed, in the hope that
God will grant them repentance leading them into a
knowledge of the truth, and that they will come to their
senses and escape from the trap of the devil, who has taken
them captive to do his will.*

2 Timothy 2:24-26

I LOVE ROSES. IT'S ONE OF MY HOBBIES AT HOME. SINCE I MOVED INTO my current home, I have been slowly expanding my rose beds. About every other year I expand the number or the types of roses I have. It provides us with beautiful flowers throughout the summer and it is one of the things that provides balance in my life. Tending roses forces you to slow down and focus. In the world of the immediate, the ever present tyranny of the urgent, having something like roses in my life helps me to come back to a place of balance.

Roses are strange things though. There are things that make them peculiar and a little harder to care for than some other flowers. In contrast, many of the flowers that line the beds around my home; (day lilies, tulips and petunias) require little to no maintenance at all. Roses just require a bit more care and attention to produce to their fullest potential.

Early in spring it is better to have more leaves than not, so sometimes you tolerate growth in a direction you don't want. Later in the season, those side branches can be trimmed back. You have to be careful doing it because if you cut too deeply early on you can stunt the growth of your roses for the entire season.

In the summer, you may need to cut branches away to open up the rose bush. There needs to be space for air to flow through the bush or disease might set in, so a branch that once produced beautiful flowers has to be cut away. In the moment it can feel counterproductive to cut something away that is vigorous, but it is necessary for the greater life of the rose.

Every season has steps to take. As winter approaches, you need to protect the roots so that future growth can occur. In some ways it looks like you are burying the rose and pruning away all life, but within that process what is really happening is that the roots down deep are preparing for another season of growth. Perhaps the greatest shift in my thinking came when I learned that protection wasn't so that the cold didn't harm the plant, but rather that it helps to keep the plant cold until it is the right time to grow. If a rose starts its growth too early then a frost can come along and kill the plant. Unfortunately, I have seen it happen.

There are so many things to learn. Fertilizer needs to be applied in certain seasons to maximize growth, but not in others because, as an example, spurring on growth as winter approaches can set the rose up for damage. Even the way a flower is cut requires attention because the place you cut the stem determines the future growth.

I joined the Louisville Rose Society a few years back and there are some absolutely masters in that group in terms of caring for roses. It's almost as if they can see the shape and the beauty of the rose bush before it even happens. They tend the rose, shape it, prune it and bring it into fullness. I am a novice compared to them. As the saying goes, a few of them have forgotten more about roses than I know. They love their roses and are so happy to share their passion with others.

As I prune my roses, there are times where multiple roses come forth from a single branch. Those roses almost never bloom at the same time. It is frustrating because that means you have to be exceptionally careful with your clippers as you go in and remove expired blooms while leaving the others that aren't quite ready yet. A steady hand is required for sure.

Now if you had to pick out a word to describe the theme of tending roses, there are a few you could choose from. For those who hate gardening in any form, there might be some choice words you would use! For me though, since I love the roses I tend, the word I would use is "gentleness."

"Gentleness" speaks of cautious and considerate action. It isn't too strong, it isn't damaging, and it doesn't leave a mark unintentionally. A gentle hand moves with a grace and a rhythm that is fully aware of the needs of its surrounding.

In the Bible the Greek word that is often used to describe gentleness is *prautes*[10]. Gentleness is sometimes defined as consideration, humility, meekness or gentle strength. Another way to think about it is gentleness is power brought under control.

When you look at gentleness in that light, the teachings of Jesus start to come into focus a little more.

> **Matthew 5:5** – "Blessed are the meek *(prautes),* for they will inherit the earth." *(Greek added)*

At first when you think about being meek, you might have thought about someone who has become a doormat and is always dominated by those around them. Too afraid to act or even scared of their environment, but that isn't the case at all.

We've all been around people who won't control what they say. If it is in, it is coming out. The problem is that lack of control damages relationships and compromises their future. There is a profound lack of gentleness in how they move through the world. Their power is out of control. The reverse also plays itself out. Some of the most successful people also have the closest guard on their speech and emotions.

If you want a picture of meekness, think of a bit put into the mouth of a horse. This tiny piece of metal allows the rider to control the movements (to stop, to turn) of the powerful horse - a thought worth considering the next time we are tempted to trample someone. It is almost cliché to exclaim, "Jesus take the wheel!" but really what we need in terms of gentleness is for us to allow Jesus to take the reins, and to pull us up before we trample those around us. To have strength under control.

To me the easiest place to see this gone wrong is over social media. There is a kind of distance with electronic media that often removes the filters on our speech. Things that we would never say to someone's face come out way faster than they ever should. It creates damage that can take months or years to overcome.

A number of years ago, my organization was ordered to move to the first floor of the same building that one of our customers resided in. We resisted the move as much as we could. We wanted our own kingdom in our own building. The downside to that kingdom was the distance between us meant there was so much more room for miscommunication and aggressive e-mails back and forth. At times the relationship between our offices was downright hostile.

After the move, what we found surprised us. We met those same people face to face on a weekly, if not daily basis. We resolved more issues face to face.

When we did have a disagreement, knowing the person you were sending an e-mail to was just down the hall tended to temper our speech. I can even remember sensing building frustration in some e-mails I was preparing to send, and instead of sending it, I moved to meet face to face, and consequently the argument lost its power. Our organizations had discovered the power of gentleness. As we brought our communications under control, our relationship grew, as did our effectiveness.

God gave us a ministry of reconciliation (2 Corinthians 5:18). Through His Son, He restored the possibility of relationship, and now we are to do the same with those that we meet. This process is not blunt, uncaring or viscous; but rather it is loving, considerate and gentle. If we are to reconcile, then we will have to deal with the hurt that comes with being around other people. We are broken people in a broken world, often doing broken things to each other. This brokenness has to be dealt with.

The position of gentleness, where all of this starts, is rooted in humility. We have all fallen short and to forget the frailty of that position is to invite pride into our lives. Even Paul, who as a Pharisee was one of the most disciplined people you would ever find, still struggled with sin.

> **Romans 7:21-25** – "We know that the law is spiritual; but I am unspiritual, sold as a slave to sin. *I do not understand what I do. For what I want to do I do not do, but what I hate I do.* And if I do what I do not want to do, I agree that the law is good. As it is, it is no longer I myself who do it, but it is sin living in me. For I know that good itself does not dwell in me, that is, in my sinful nature. *For I have the desire to do what is good, but I cannot carry it out. For I do not do the good I want to do, but the evil I do not want to do—this I keep on doing.* Now if I do what I do not want to do, it is no longer I who do it, but it is sin living in me that does it.

So I find this law at work: *Although I want to do good, evil is right there with me.* For in my inner being I delight in God's law; but I see another law at work in me, waging war against the law of my mind and making me a prisoner of the law of sin at work within me. What a wretched man I am! Who will rescue me from this body that is subject to death? Thanks be to God, who delivers me through Jesus Christ our Lord!" *(Emphasis added.)*

The question then has to be asked - how would you want God to deal with your sin? My guess is that the answer at least on some level would be answered – gently. How then are we to deal with the sins of others? Gently. This process of correcting and pruning has to be done thoughtfully and carefully. We are called to treat our neighbors as ourselves after all.

2 Timothy 2:25-26 – "Opponents must be gently instructed, in the hope that God will grant them repentance leading them to a knowledge of the truth, and that they will come to their senses and escape from the trap of the devil, who has taken them captive to do his will."

Galatians 6:1 – "Brothers, if anyone is caught in any transgression, you who are spiritual should restore him in a spirit of gentleness. Keep watch on yourself, lest you too be tempted."

A way that you can identify mature Christians is by the way they deal with the sins of another. Love is patient, love is kind. It does not envy, it does not boast, it is not proud. It does not dishonor others (1 Corinthians 13:4-5). All of those aspects of love speak to gentleness. Where actions are taken, especially in public forums, to dishonor another you can be sure that the spirit of God is not present.

In any situation, it is always a good idea to find out what Jesus said about a topic. As a perfect representation of God to us, His words carry the demand to stand as He stood, and view the world from His perspective.

> **Matthew 18:15-17 -** "If your brother or sister sins, go and point out their fault, just between the two of you. If they listen to you, you have won them over. But if they will not listen, take one or two others along, so that 'every matter may be established by the testimony of two or three witnesses.' If they still refuse to listen, tell it to the church; and if they refuse to listen even to the church, treat them as you would a pagan or a tax collector."

This verse has been used over the years to exclude people from the Church, but it is worth remembering that the author of the book (Matthew) was a tax collector. They also were spoken by Jesus, who was often criticized for spending time with unrepentant sinners of various kinds (Matthew 9:10-12). This isn't a call to cut off, but a call to double down on relationships. It is a call to gentle and intentional action.

Additionally, reading any passage in the Bible would be incomplete without a study of context. Some of that study is the history and cultural significance of the actions and words being spoken, but some of it is simply seeing the passages as a narrative whole and reading where the scriptures are set in relation to each other. This set of passages are book ended by two powerful stories that flavor the way we should read those words Jesus spoke.

The parable of the wandering sheep sets the tone.

> **Matthew 18:10-14** - "See that you do not despise one of these little ones. For I tell you that their angels in heaven always see the face of my Father in heaven. "What do you think? If a man owns a hundred sheep, and one of them wanders away, will he not leave the ninety-nine on the hills and go to look for the one that wandered off? And if he finds it, truly I tell you, he is happier about that one sheep than about the ninety-nine that did not wander off. In the same way your Father in heaven is not willing that any of these little ones should perish."

You don't even have to leave the church pew to wander, but whether you have left in a physical or spiritual sense, we are to seek the lost, just as He did for us.

Following those passages Jesus tells the parable of the unmerciful servant.

> **Matthew 18:21-35** – "Then Peter came to Jesus and asked, 'Lord, how many times shall I forgive my brother or sister who sins against me? Up to seven times?' Jesus answered, 'I tell you, not seven times, but seventy-seven times. Therefore, the kingdom of heaven is like a king who wanted to settle accounts with his servants. As he began the settlement, a man who owed him ten thousand bags of gold was brought to him. Since he was not able to pay, the master ordered that he and his wife and his children and all that he had be sold to repay the debt.' At this the servant fell on his knees before him. 'Be patient with me,' he begged, 'and I will pay back everything.' The servant's master took pity on

him, canceled the debt and let him go. But when that servant went out, he found one of his fellow servants who owed him a hundred silver coins. He grabbed him and began to choke him. 'Pay back what you owe me!' he demanded. His fellow servant fell to his knees and begged him, 'Be patient with me, and I will pay it back.' But he refused. Instead, he went off and had the man thrown into prison until he could pay the debt. When the other servants saw what had happened, they were outraged and went and told their master everything that had happened. Then the master called the servant in. 'You wicked servant,' he said, 'I canceled all that debt of yours because you begged me to. Shouldn't you have had mercy on your fellow servant just as I had on you?' In anger his master handed him over to the jailers to be tortured, until he should pay back all he owed. 'This is how my heavenly Father will treat each of you unless you forgive your brother or sister from your heart.'"

That passage speaks loudly that we are to forgive as we have been forgiven.

When you look at the balance of those three passages it leads us to a remarkable conclusion about how we are to treat one another. We are to go find the lost, we are to do that in relationship, and we are to bring a spirit of humility as we forgive those who sinned, because we have sinned as well. Those are radical beliefs that continue to shake the world to this day because they are so counter cultural.

Gentleness certainly doesn't mean abandoning truth, but it does inform the way that we wield that truth. When we use truth as a weapon, we join the enemy in his work. Yes, truth is sharper than any two edged sword (Hebrews

4:12), but it is to be used as a surgeon's scalpel, removing the cancer but not endangering the life of the patient. Pruning people, just as with roses, takes a delicate and careful touch.

Love protects, just as much as it trusts and hopes (1 Corinthians 13:7), so there are times that exclusion is necessary to protect the vulnerable. Those decisions require incredible amounts of wisdom and should only be carried out after extensive prayer and counsel. There certainly is tension between trust, hope and protection. Living in that tensions is an absolute necessity to the active Christian life. It is the tensioned string that propels the arrow, and it is God's wisdom that helps us to aim that arrow and hit the mark in any situation.

> **Proverbs 9:10** – "The fear of the Lord is the beginning of wisdom, and knowledge of the Holy One is understanding."

Redemption and reconciliation are the missions we have set before us. Our actions, when put together, should produce a harmony that reflects gentleness. It is the "default setting" that Scripture indicates we should take with our actions. Our power brought under control for the redemption and restoration of others.

To put that another way, when someone comes to mind who is wandering from the faith, can you imagine that person reconciled and drawn back? Can you imagine a useful and honored place at the table of Jesus? If you do not have a redemptive solution in mind for a person, then you don't have a full solution. The Bible commands us that the most effective way to affect change is through gentleness.

A woman caught in the act of adultery was brought before Jesus (John 8:1-11). The law defined the punishment that was to be given to her for this sin, which was to be stoned to death. (Important to note it also defined the same punishment for the man, but he is no-where to be found. – Leviticus 20:10). Among other things I would say the response that Jesus gave personifies "gentle." He didn't condemn. He simply urged her to leave her life of sin. This was power brought under control. If anyone who has ever lived had the right to swing a sword, it was Jesus, yet He didn't.

There is something truly disorienting about His reaction when we think about it. How would you react if you were sinned against in that way? Would your first reaction be a gentle one? Most likely not. When we experience reactions and behaviors that don't match our actions, it is disorienting and moves our hearts. We have all experienced that in a negative way, where we received evil for the good we did. Those moments can leave deep scars. That said, it can be just as disorienting and transformational when we respond to evil with good.

A gentle answer turns away wrath (Proverbs 15:1) and it can also break something inside of us (Proverbs 25:15) that is necessary for change and for us to live in the fullness that God created us for.

Gentleness truly demonstrates strength brought under control. It is the key to the redemption and restoration of others. Where do you need to show gentleness today?

For Further Reflection...

1. How does society define being gentle or meek?

2. Why is it so hard to give a gentle answer in the face of anger?

3. What ways can we practically express gentleness in our everyday lives?

4. Should we expect people to change if we exclude them?

5. When is that necessary?

6. Can you imagine a fully redeemed and reconciled future for someone who is lost that you know?

7. What steals our gentleness?

Gentleness one of the keys to transformation. Gentleness speaks to humility, in that people and their problems are often very complicated and require God's wisdom to resolve. It is also about meekness, which is power brought under control. Just because we have the authority to proverbially stone someone, doesn't mean we should.

Gentleness takes time. It is a slow moving stream that carves a canyon, and it takes time to do its work. For that we need something else, for that we need...

CHAPTER 10

Self-Control

For God gave us a spirit not of fear but of power, love and
self-control.

2 Timothy 1:7 (ESV)

W E HAVE AN EMMAUS COMMUNITY IN ELIZABETHTOWN,
Kentucky. It is a wonderful group of people committed to serving
Jesus. I love the fact that people from many churches, different races, backgrounds and economic conditions all come together to serve our community
and each other.

When entering into the Emmaus Community, there is a process to go
through, usually over an extended weekend, where you learn more about discipleship, the character of Jesus and the mission we are on this world to serve.
It was a fantastic experience for me. There are certainly moments within that
weekend that I will never forget.

What you don't realize while you are in the middle of the experience is
the number of people around you who are serving in the background in order
to make it a reality. You come into contact with some of the people who are

serving the food, but in many ways, even at the end, you don't appreciate the full width and depth of the effort it takes to make the weekend what it is.

Some years after I did my walk and entered the Emmaus Community, I had a chance to serve. I had been asked a few times before but work had gotten in the way with business travel and such. This time, I had the opportunity and the time so I protected my calendar fiercely.

I am really glad I ended up serving. I worked with a group of men who were as committed to Jesus as any I have ever met. The experience for the pilgrims (the name given to the people who enter the walk) was outstanding, and there was certainly a greater purpose served.

I was asked later about whether I had a great time and whether it was worth it. The answer I gave seemed to surprise many.

No, it wasn't a great time, but it absolutely was worth it.

If I am being completely honest with you, the weekend wasn't a lot of fun. Yes, I got to meet and serve with some great guys as I said. That much is absolutely true. That said, spending a weekend working *really* hard cleaning toilets, sweeping, taking out trash, mopping up messes and tidying up the living spaces of a bunch of men isn't exactly my idea of a great time. You don't have to imagine the work very long - cleaning up after a bunch of men - before the mystique and excitement wears off.

Does that mean it wasn't worth it? Certainly not! It was absolutely worth it. I am glad I spent the time that way. Serving obediently to the body of Christ is never a waste of time. It always has purpose - whether you can see it or not. And I would absolutely do it again. And to be transparent; the people who asked me to serve were very clear on the front side of the mission about what was going to be expected of me and how hard we were going to work. I wasn't duped into serving, and I went into it with my eyes wide open.

The thing is, we aren't always going to feel like serving. We aren't always going to be energized by the work we have in front of us. For those instances we need discipline. For those instances we need focus and determination. For those instances we need self-control.

When we talk about our church, we often talk of it in terms of being a family. I certainly get that. There are people who are closer to me within my church than some of my extended family. I share with them my joys, struggles, victories and my defeats. I am truly thankful for them. The thing is, just like our own families, there is work that needs to be done that doesn't exactly excite you.

At least in my family, there isn't a single one of us that is anointed in a special way to take out the trash. Maybe I should have had more kids. Maybe then, at some point one day, someone would have woken up with a special gifting and anointing to take out the garbage from our home. That person could lead a great national movement to help others "discover" this gift. Probably wasn't going to happen. I think my wife would have gotten tired of having kids WAY before that would have ever happened.

That fact of the matter is that no one is anointed to take out the trash. That's not why you do it. You do it because you don't want your house to stink. You're not always going to feel like doing it. Our emotions are wonderful servants, but they are terrible masters. When our feelings serve our overall goals and the work we do, it can be an amazing experience and truly transformative. That said, whether we feel like doing the right things or not, they are still the right things to do.

Much of the teaching on self-control is focused on what not to do. Self-control is viewed as some spiritual version of having the restraint needed to not eat the entire chocolate cake in one sitting, or to not throw an apple core at your sister's head while she is driving. (My failures on complete display.) Just as important is the willingness to do what is right despite your feelings to do otherwise.

As has been the case throughout the book, the perfect representation of this fruit is Jesus. There is no greater display of self-control than the moments before he went to the cross.

> **Luke 22:39-44** – "Jesus went out as usual to the Mount of Olives, and his disciples followed him. On reaching the place, he said to them, 'Pray that you will not fall into temptation.' He withdrew about a stone's throw beyond them, knelt down and prayed, "Father, if you are willing, take this cup from me; yet not my will, but yours be done." An angel from heaven appeared to him and strengthened him. And being in anguish, he prayed more earnestly, and his sweat was like drops of blood falling to the ground."

Jesus knew the brutal experience that was in front of Him. Huge nails would be driven through His hands and feet. Those open wounds would be the places where His body would come in contact with the cross. Eventually when His muscles were worn out, His shoulders would dislocate. His back would have been lashed to the point that most of the skin had been mangled, ribs and cartilage exposed. The Romans used the cross as a symbol of power, humiliation and intimidation to all who witnessed it. It is unbelievably brutal. I would submit to you then that an equally unbelievable amount of self-control would be necessary to walk into that willingly. Know this: no one put Him on that cross. He went there willingly for you and me.

> **Hebrews 12:2** – "For the joy set before Him he endured the cross, scorning its shame, and sat down at the right hand of the throne of God."

In His prayer to God the Father you can sense the turmoil. It as if He is saying – if there is ANY other way this can be done, let's do it! In the end though, the self-control He displayed in order to go through with something that God had set before Him led to arguably the greatest moment in human history.

Self-control is something that doesn't normally result in our immediate benefit. It isn't always going to feel good. It isn't always going to be recognized. It is important nevertheless. Doing only the things we feel like doing is the smooth and comfortable road to apathy and atrophy. This applies to our spiritual walk, our work, and our relationships.

There are many times when doing the right thing makes our lives more complicated, harder and more expensive. This can clearly be seen in Jesus's life as He heals a man with leprosy.

> **Mark 1:40-45** – "A man with leprosy came to Him and begged Him on his knees, 'If you are willing, you can make me clean.' Jesus was indignant. He reached out His hand and touched the man. 'I am willing,' He said. 'Be clean!' Immediately the leprosy left him and he was cleansed. Jesus sent him away at once with a strong warning: 'See that you don't tell this to anyone. But go, show yourself to the priest and offer the sacrifices that Moses commanded for your cleansing, as a testimony to them.' Instead he went out and began to talk freely, spreading the news. As a result, Jesus could no longer enter a town openly but stayed outside in lonely places. Yet the people still came to Him from everywhere."

There may have been many reasons for Jesus to say that to the man, but I think at least part of this is the difficulty and complications He knew it would bring. It is like He is saying, "Kid, listen to me. Don't tell anyone about this. Please. It is going to make my work SO MUCH HARDER if you tell everyone about what I have done for you." God's heart was to heal the man. Whether He was obedient afterwards had nothing to do with what the right thing to do was in Jesus's mind. He was going to heal. He was going to do the right thing. That didn't reverse what He knew was going to happen. In this powerful moment of self-control displayed the entire paradigm of how the people of God were to live changed. Before this moment, if something unclean touched you, you were unclean and to be cut off (Leviticus 11:8). Now with Jesus, and by extension with the Holy Spirit living in us, He demonstrated that when He touches what is unclean, it becomes clean. What an incredible gift born out of a moment of self-control!

Those moments of self-control are important because they set the broader course for our lives. Sometimes they are tests placed in front of us as gates to determine if we are ready to handle greater levels of blessing and the responsibility that goes with them. Sometimes they are gifts that change the lives of people around us. In neither of those cases does it mean that our lives become easier. It is still the right thing to do.

There are times when the emotions and feelings are right there with us at the beginning of a process. They may fade over time, and our choices suffer. There is a clear description of what it looks like when that happens to the church in Ephesus.

> **Revelation 2:2-5** – "I know your deeds, your hard work and your perseverance. I know you cannot tolerate wicked people, that you have tested those who claim to be apostles but are not, and have found them false. You have persevered and have endured hardships for my name, and have not grown weary. Yet I hold this against you: You have forsaken the love you had at first. Consider how far you have fallen! Repent and do the things you did at first. If you do not repent, I will come to you and remove your lampstand from its place."

There is an indication with the church that there is something they used to do but now are choosing not to do it. They aren't weary, so they aren't physically incapable of doing it, but they are simply choosing not to.

Around the New Year, so many people resolve to exercise more. It is part of a broader goal of getting into better shape and living a healthier lifestyle. I've done it more than a few times myself. When you come into a gym the first few weeks of January the gym is full of eager and fresh faces doing great work. There is even real progress; weight is being lost, strength and tone are being gained. It is great to see!

Then something else begins to happen. Soreness sets in. Achieving new milestones take much longer. The newness of the activity has worn off and now the clear road in front of each person is set before them. They can see what has to be done to get to the next level, but the question has to be asked about whether or not they will choose to do it? And even if they do choose to do what is right in the gym, a moment outside of the gym (see the previous reference about eating an entire chocolate cake in one sitting) can derail an entire week's worth of work. It can be frustrating to say the least, but this is where self-control must assert itself.

In our relationships, our work, and our spiritual lives we can ask the very same questions. Where have we lost our first love? What did we once do that we don't do anymore? I am guessing you know exactly what it is. I don't know what that is for you. Each of us is different; but is there something standing in the way of where you want to be in your relationships, work and spiritual lives? I would wager that progress begins with a moment of choice, a moment of self-control. Is that thing going to make your life a little harder, a little more complex? Perhaps, but is it the right thing to do?

Early in the churches history, there is a really curious moment with Peter. He has a vision (see Acts 10) where he is told by God to do things that at the time were viewed as a sin, namely by eating animals that were ceremonially unclean. Peter vigorously argues with the Lord. When you read the passage it is pretty clear that Peter is having a really hard time accepting the word given. The Spirit even describes to him that three men were looking for him, to get up and go downstairs, and not to hesitate to go with them since He has sent them (Acts 10:19-20).

So what does Peter do? He doesn't leave until the next morning. (So much for "do not hesitate.") Part of this was the confusing vision. Part of this is that he is being sent to a Centurion of the Roman Army. I am guessing that the majority of times Peter encountered members of the Roman Army, they probably were not positive experiences. Yet here was God calling Peter to go to a Gentile. To a Roman Gentile. To a Roman Centurion Gentile. This was a moment of self-control.

Peter went the next day. What came out of this meeting would eventually be the inclusion of the Gentiles (non-Jewish people) into the body of the Church. The gospel wasn't meant to be exclusive to the Jewish people. God had lifted Peter's eyes and now he more fully understood the mission the God had given to him.

This moment of self-control proved itself to be greater than race, greater than orthodoxy, greater than mistrust, and greater than hundreds of years of history. This moment of self-control continues to multiply and grow each time a believer is brought into relationship with Jesus.

This certainly doesn't mean things got easier for the Church in Peter's day, much like it continues to this day. Each time we blend cultures, races and extended age groups our lives become a little more complex and harder. The result is a far richer life, just as Jesus promised to us.

Self-control is the fruit we must pick off the vine ourselves. When we lay our lives down and accept Jesus as Lord, what in reality we are saying is that His values, wisdom and decisions are best. We do not rely on our own understanding, but rather rely on His (Proverbs 3:5).

It has been said that everything we want in life is on the other side of our fears. While I think that is true, I would further clarify that almost everything we want in life; for ourselves, our families, our work, relationships or spiritual life, is on the other side of self-control. Self-control is key because it involves every other aspect of the Fruit of the Spirit.

The choice to follow what God says, despite how we may feel, is a pathway to blessing for us and for those around us. It may not be easy. It may not make our lives simpler. But it is always worth it.

What will you chose today?

For Further Reflection...

1. How does self-control relate to the other fruit of the Spirit?

2. What areas of your life do you find it hardest to exert self-control?

3. What is the outcome when we don't exert self-control?

4. Does what we feel make a choice any less right or wrong?

5. We take out the garbage not because we are anointed, but because we don't want our house to stink. What areas of your life do you need to apply that concept to?

6. Is self-control stolen from us or is it a choice not to use it?

Self-control is necessary in our lives if we are ever to get where God wants us to be. Those choices demonstrate our priorities and who has Lordship in our lives.

The fruit of the Spirit is important and critical to our walk as Christians. The fruit doesn't happen by accident through, and if we are to produce much fruit, something else is needed. For that, we need to...

Part 2
Abide

John 15:5-8 (ESV) - "I am the vine; you are the branches. *Whoever abides in me and I in him, he it is that bears much fruit, for apart from me you can do nothing.* If anyone does not abide in me he is thrown away like a branch and withers; and the branches are gathered, thrown into the fire, and burned. If you abide in me, and my words abide in you, ask whatever you wish, and it will be done for you. *By this my Father is glorified, that you bear much fruit and so prove to be my disciples*" *(Emphasis added).*

CHAPTER 11

The Good Shepherd

I am the good shepherd; I know my sheep and my sheep know me – just as the Father knows me and I know the Father – and I lay down my life for the sheep.

John 10:14-15

I HAD A LAPTOP A FEW YEARS BACK THAT WAS EASILY ONE OF THE BEST I have owned. It was a great computer, super portable, extremely reliable and had a great battery life. The keyboard just seemed to 'fit' me if that makes sense. Sometimes they can be too small, sometimes oddly large for the computer. This one was the "Goldilocks" version.

There was one other thing I always thought was neat about it as well. The computer power cord had a little blue light at the end of it as part of where it plugged into the laptop itself. That way you could easily tell when it was plugged in and you were getting power. It comes in handy, especially in group settings where you are running off of an extension cord, when you aren't sure if everything is hooked up.

One day I noticed something else. I was on business travel and in my hotel room, packing things up in the morning, getting ready to leave for the week and pulled the plug on the cord. In the mornings I tend to keep the light in my room fairly muted, so what I found next surprised me. The little blue light at the end of the power cord stayed on even though it wasn't plugged in. Turns out there was a capacitor in the power cord that not only protects from power surges, but also provided consistent power for a short period of time. The little blue light stayed on for a surprisingly long time, softly glowing in my bag, even though it wasn't hooked to the source. After a while, the blue light faded and was once again dark.

People are a lot like that. We go to worship on Sunday, plug in and the light shines bright. However if we only rely on Sunday worship and then unplug on Monday our little light is going to fade. Sunday worship is a great thing, no doubt. Our town is blessed to have a bunch of amazing churches that provide a great environment for worship, community, Scripture and a solid sermon every week. Sunday church services are a vital piece of our Christian walk, it just can't be the only thing we do if we expect to be able to bear much fruit. It's got to be more.

> **John 15:5-8 (ESV)** - "I am the vine; you are the branches. *Whoever abides in me and I in him, he it is that bears much fruit, for apart from me you can do nothing.* If anyone does not abide in me he is thrown away like a branch and withers; and the branches are gathered, thrown into the fire, and burned. If you abide in me, and my words abide in you, ask whatever you wish, and it will be done for you. *By this my Father is glorified, that you bear much fruit and so prove to be my disciples*" (Emphasis added).

When I read that Scripture, I think about what it practically means to "abide." We've already seen how valuable the fruit is that Jesus is referring to; but now the challenge before us is to abide. It isn't as if you can put that on the top of your "to do" list and know exactly what's next. It is a word, but so much more is wrapped inside. It is a theme *and* a lifestyle.

Some Bible translations define abide: to remain or to dwell with. It speaks to an intimate, life giving relationship that flows out of connection. Sure, but that isn't exactly helping me get to the practical either.

It reminds me of something you might hear in a business conference. We need to have an action bias, think out of the box, while proactively attacking our problems. They might all be great concepts, but where do you practically begin with each of them?

What I really want is a checklist. (It might be that this is just one more area of my Army experience coming out in me.) I love checklists because they help to make sure that as I move through life I remember the basic elements of success. In life you may find yourself tired or stressed, and in those moments it is great to have something like a checklist to lean on and help you.

On some level I can almost hear the gasps! You can't reduce a relationship to a checklist! Especially one with God! That's true on a certain level. Just because I perform a certain set of tasks in no way guarantees an outcome or that you will even have a relationship. The heart with which you do anything absolutely matters. That said, if you are seeking a better relationship with God and looking to produce more fruit, your heart probably isn't the issue.

In any relationship or effort there are basics to success. Those basics are foundational actions, that if you perform correctly, will go a long way to giving you success. As an example for the married readers - do you spend at least 30 minutes a day having a meaningful conversation with your spouse? (Family coordination meetings don't count.) Do you forgive and are you willing to ask forgiveness for what you have done wrong? Do you regularly pray for your spouse? Do you look to serve your spouse in ways that are meaningful to them? (Rather than meaningful for you.) Do you regularly encourage your spouse?

If you do those five things regularly out of heart for your spouse's benefit then I am going to go out on a limb and say you have a really healthy chance at a solid marriage. Can things still go wrong? Sure, but basics aren't meant to be an exhaustive list but rather a solid base from which to start and build from.

So can we find a similar set of basics that will help us to abide? As I began to study this question a connection occurred to me. Jesus has seven "I am" statements that He made throughout His time on Earth. For example He said "I am the bread of life" in John 6:35. He also said "I am the way, the truth, and the life" in John 14:6.

The one I would like to particularly focus on is in John 10:11 where He says "I am the Good Shepherd." It is out of this concept that we can take our first steps in learning what it means to abide. He is our Shepherd. We are His flock. Abiding means being a good sheep of the Good Shepherd. That may seem elementary to you, but on some level that is what a basic is. It is a building block that keys you towards success.

With that said, what better place to start than the Shepherd's prayer in Psalm 23.

> **Psalm 23:1-6** – "The Lord is my shepherd, I lack nothing. He makes me lie down in green pastures, he leads me beside quiet waters, He refreshes my soul. He guides me along the right paths for his name's sake. Even though I walk through the darkest valley, I will fear no evil, for you are with me; your rod and your staff, they comfort me. You prepare a table for me in the presence of my enemies. You anoint my head with oil; my cup overflows. Surely your goodness and love

will follow me all the days of my life, and I will dwell in the house of the Lord forever."

Out of this Psalm we can see some basics, when you look at them through the eyes of the sheep, to abiding well with God. Some of it requires a basic understanding of shepherding culture, but none of it is outside of our grasp.

The first point in the Psalm is the statement that "The Lord is my shepherd, I lack nothing." Is that how you live? Are you living in such a way that you can be content with what God has brought to your life, or when you don't perceive you are getting what you want, do you wander? The shepherd provides everything needed for the flock. God does the same for us if we allow it.

Don't mistake what I am saying as an excuse not to be ambitious. Many of the things God wants for us will take a tremendous amount of work to achieve – whether that is a ministry, relationship, or a financial goal. Working hard and being ambitious isn't a bad thing at all as long as it is aligned with God's values. Where we get in trouble is when we leave the care of the shepherd by taking shortcuts or going outside of God's commands and laws to achieve our ends. Much as we said earlier in Chapter 7 when we focused on Goodness, the enemy doesn't care about what cause you believe in, as long as you leave the character of Christ to defend it or achieve it. When we do that we sin, possibly compromising our witness, future, and the protection and provision of the Shepherd.

To put it another way, God's laws are there as a virtual fence for us. What does that fence look like to you? Does it look like a fence keeping you away from what you really want? From fun, success, and resource? Or is the fence something that is there to protect you from the lions and the bears who are looking to devour you on the other side? When we think we know better and we strive to put something in our hands that God hasn't given to us, it can cost us much more than we ever imagined. Stay close and be content with what the Shepherd provides you.

The second piece of this deals with the verse about "green pastures." Where I live you can almost hear the grass grow it comes up so fast in the spring. The warmer temperatures and plentiful rain make it so you almost have to cut your grass every four days or it will get too high to mow. With that kind of background it is tempting to think of "green pastures" as ankle deep alfalfa that you would never have to move from as a sheep. The context David would have known in Israel is much different. The land that has that kind of rain was almost exclusively used for farming crops rather than tending sheep. When you look at the land that Middle Eastern farmers use to feed their flocks you wonder how that kind of land can support anything at all. In the southern part of the country the wind out of the Mediterranean Sea brings just enough humidity with it to create condensation on the rocks which drips water for small tufts of grass to form. To them, these areas were "green pasture." It is a place where we walk with the Good Shepherd and He brings us into daily provision.

So if we flip that around to the sheep's perspective, are we willing to walk daily with our Shepherd? Just like a relationship with another person, if you only talk to the person once a week the relationship will only be so deep and only so fruitful. To abide well, our relationship with the Good Shepherd is one where we must interact and walk with Him daily. If we do that we can trust that He will bring us to places of daily provision that will sustain us for the day. Worry in so many ways is trying to imagine solving tomorrow's problems with only today's provision. So whether that is prayer time, reading Scripture or listening to a sermon podcast, take the time daily to interact with God. Walking with the Shepherd daily will bring you into a place of provision.

The third aspect to bring up is where "He leads me beside quiet waters." What is interesting to me is that the word "quiet", sometimes translated as "rest," is a noun and at the end of the sentence in Hebrew.[11] "Waters of rest," as it is literally written, has a different feel to it. It speaks to a place where you find refreshment, rest and a quietness inside.

Modern life has so many demands to it. We have family, school, and work obligations. In our homes the TV's are on just to provide background noise. The news is troubling, the internet and social media is worse, and it all leaves us feeling taxed to our limits. Like our computer is on, we have twenty three browser tabs open, half of them aren't responding and you have no idea where the music is coming from. Can anyone else relate?

What are we to do? Are we willing to let the Good Shepherd lead us to a place of rest? Where do you find that rest with God? At least for me, the places I find that kind of rest are in places like corporate worship, service, and in the company of mature believers. So many people view those three as burdens, but I can't imagine living without them.

Something about worship reorients my heart. The old saying about – quit telling God about the size of your problem and start telling your problem about the size of your God – has some validity to it. When we worship God comes into clearer focus. It doesn't take away our problems, but it does put them in their proper orientation. Putting my problems, desires, issues and challenges into their proper perspective is a giant step towards peace.

Service is another thing that brings me an inner rest. Yes, the work I do in service may tax and sometimes wear down the physical body I have, but when we serve someone in love then there is a refreshment to our soul that comes with it.

I also have friends who just seem to carry peace with them everywhere they go. As I mentioned before, I pray with a great couple, Jeff and Vanessa Swisher, as a service to our church. I have been to their home a few times to pray and worship. When I entered their home, it just felt like a place of peace. I am sure from time to time that is interrupted, as all of our homes do from time to time, but being in community with wise and mature believers brings you peace and refreshment.

The Psalms close with a call to worship. "Let everything that has breath praise the Lord." (Psalm 150:6) Christ exclaims: "The greatest among you will be your servant" Matthew 23:11. Paul exhorts: "And let us consider how we may spur one another on toward love and good deeds, not giving up meeting together, as some are in the habit of doing, but encouraging one another – and all the more as you see the day approaching" (Romans 10:24-25).

Those commands aren't there just to keep us busy. I once viewed worship, fellowship with believers, and the study of Scripture as obligations and even perhaps as a test of loyalty from God. In reality they are the things He placed in my life to give me peace, refreshment and rest. The question then becomes, are you willing to follow the lead of the Good Shepherd? When our view shifts away from obligation to opportunity, our lives can be transformed. Follow the Good Shepherd to rest.

The fourth fundamental we see is about the character of God. "He guides me along the right paths for His name's sake," and "You prepare a table before me in the presence of my enemies." For us to do each of those well we have to trust the character of the Good Shepherd. He wants us to trust Him. He leads us for our safety because He loves us, but don't miss that God cares about the reputation that He has with us.

When we allow Him to have the authority to lead and guide our decisions then it will lead us into a place of provision. If you did what He told you to do and it led you to ruin, what effect would that have on His reputation? Would you continue to trust in Him? How about those around you?

Following God doesn't keep us from all trouble: "I have told you these things, so that in me you may have peace. In this world you will have trouble. But take heart! I have overcome the world" John 16:33. Following God is still the best path forward. Remember that there is a big difference between easier and easy. By following God and His wisdom we make our lives much easier, but that doesn't mean it will be easy. Each time we trust God and follow His wisdom we are brought into a more spacious place than we left. That could be physically, spiritually or mentally. He does this for His name's sake.

As we move through those times of trouble there will be moments where we are called to trust. Every one of us has things in our lives that are long term prayers. It might be the salvation of others we are praying for, success of a ministry or business venture, or the establishment or expansion of your family. Whatever it is, as we work through the months and sometimes years of waiting God prepares a table for us in the presence of the things that oppose us.

In Hebrew, the word for "enemy" is actually a verb, so it is meant represent the things that are actively opposing us and hemming us in.[12] The table is meant to sustain us until we come to that place of final victory and peace. It is worth remembering that just because He sets the table doesn't mean we automatically eat! That is our decision to trust His character. That is our decision to be nourished along the way as we move towards fulfilling the promises and purposes of God in our lives.

My dog has this habit that breaks my heart at times. One of the first things he does after greeting me is go after his food with gusto. The thing is, that food has been there all day. He's just been too nervous to eat because, apparently, he wasn't sure I was coming home, didn't feel safe, or felt abandoned. It truly saddens me when I think about it. I've thought about ways to fix that, but the Government tends to frown on people bringing their pets to work. I wonder about what else I have to do to get my dog to trust me. Every day he has food and water. Every day he has a place of rest. Every day he gets treats, pets, and rubs from his family. Yet he still worries.

I shake my head about it, but when it comes down to it, most of us are no different. It takes surprisingly little for us to start worrying. On some levels it must break the heart of God to provide and love us as He does, only to have us paralyzed by worry. The feast that God has set out for us goes uneaten, and we continue to worry about the things that are resisting us, when in reality if we trusted the Good Shepherd, then we would eat and be strengthened for the journey to come.

In a practical sense, one way you can do this every week is to go to Sunday worship. We all bring our fears, problems, thoughts, failures and addictions in with us. Don't ever think you are alone in your struggle. The enemy won't leave you alone, no matter what row or pew you sit in. In a very real sense, these are the things that oppose us. They are the enemies that want to keep us from the destiny God has in store for us. Whether it is by worship or Holy Communion, God has set a table for us in the presence of those things. So yes, in the presence of cancer, in the presence of depression, in the presence of crisis, whatever it is; we get to worship. We get to come to the table. When we chose to do those things, it is an act of defiance where we look to the powers of hell and remind them that they will not have the final say.[13] When the enemy tries to remind us of our past, we worship as a way to remind him of his future. It is a place where by our trust in the Good Shepherd we are sustained until the victory is won. Trust His character.

The fifth and final basic we can learn, "Your rod and your staff, they comfort me." Are you willing to accept God's protection? Are you willing to accept His discipline? Both of those are deliberate decisions that we have to make in our lives.

Proverbs 2:7 says "He holds success in store for the upright, He is a shield to those whose walk is blameless." Accepting the protection of the shepherd means coming to Him in prayer and following the wisdom that is revealed. We balance that revelation with the Scriptures to make sure that what we are following is consistent. When you think you know better than God, you don't. When we come into agreement with Him, there is success stored up for us.

None of us do this correctly all the time. Even the best of intentions still fail. It is part of our broken nature. That is where the other aspect of this portion of Scripture applies. When we do wrong there are consequences that God often brings into our lives. It isn't about losing our salvation, which is secure in Christ, but rather a way that He guides us. The shepherd's staff is sometimes used to grab the sheep and pull them back onto a different path or to provide a tap on the rear to get going.

Hebrews 12:6 – "Because the Lord disciplines the one He loves, and He chastens everyone He accepts as His son."

No matter what age we are, discipline is not easy to accept, especially when we are the middle of disobedience. Repentance, or turning away from what we are doing, is the first step. As the old saying goes – Do you know what the first step of getting out of a hole is? Quit digging. When we quit digging the hole we are making for ourselves, accept the discipline and wisdom of God, then we are on the road to better. Accept His protection and discipline.

Those five basics - Stay close and be content with what the Shepherd provides you, walk with the Shepherd daily into a place of provision, follow the Good Shepherd to rest and refreshment, trust in His character and accept His protection and discipline – are a great place to start in our journey to abide well with God, and in turn producing fruit.

It is amazing to me to realize that David saw the same thing around 3,000 years before Christ declared the relationship between abiding and producing fruit. When David did those fundamental things well, what followed him all the days of his life? Goodness and love. When David trusted in God, walking as he did through the darkest of valley's in his life, he didn't fear evil. That is faithfulness and peace. And even in the years while he was running from Saul he still found places of provision and trust in God's character. He had moments where he could have shortcut the process by killing King Saul himself, but it would have been in disobedience to God. He followed God and spared Saul's life in those moments. That is patience that continues to be faithful in the presence of the enemies he faced.

He is the Good Shepherd. When we abide we will produce fruit. Nothing will ever change that. The real question is, will we be the good sheep of His flock?

For Further Reflection...

1. Is He the Good Shepherd? How do you know?

2. What fundamentals do you follow as you walk out your faith?

3. How do you balance being content and being ambitious for the things God wants for you in your life?

4. What are practical things you can do for daily relationship with God?

5. Why do we worry so much in the presence of the Good Shepherd?

6. What practical ways do you use to eat at the table that God has set for you in the presence of your enemies?

7. Why is it so hard to accept discipline?

8. Can you think of moments where you produced fruit in your life? Were they tied to moments where you abided well with God?

CHAPTER 12

Our Guest & Host

*I pray that out of His glorious riches He may strengthen
you with power through His Spirit in your inner being,
so that Christ may dwell in your hearts through faith.*

Ephesians 3:16-17

JUST ABOUT ALL OF US HAVE SOME EXPERIENCE BEING A GUEST IN someone else's home. Think back to those experiences - were you a good guest? I had a friend when I was in middle school, Dustin, whose Dad was an amazing pool player. We had to make up rules for him to make the games competitive. He would play with us down in their basement on what was a spectacularly nice pool table. One day when I was using the bridge I hit a shot and the ball was coming back at the bridge fast so I lifted it up really quick to get it up and out of the way – right into the lamp that was over the pool table. I broke the bulb, and it sent glass shards everywhere. Let's just say I could have been a better guest that day.

Have you ever been a guest in someone's home and they were a bad host? The food wasn't good, they didn't give you an extra blanket so you were cold all night, or maybe they just were barely willing to have you even there. There are so many ways that can go wrong. I've experienced a few of those as I am sure you have.

How about those times when you were the host? What did you do to make it comfortable for the people who came to your home? I love to cook so when people come to my home I really try to at least have one meal that is special for them. Of course, that varies a great deal based upon the guests we had over. When my son was in his early teens and had all of his friends over "special" meant as much pizza as they could eat. With my son's wife's family it is my spaghetti, mounds of freshly grated Reggiano Parmesan and baked bread right out of the oven. I want that meal to make them feel as warm and as special as I know they are.

And yes, I wish it weren't the case, but there have been times where I was less than the best host. Periods of time where I was stressed out from work, tired or just plain grumpy with the guests I had. All of it resulted in times where my guests barely felt they were a guest at all. I am lucky that when those times come, (and they aren't often) my wife is there to pick up the slack for me.

This relationship of guest and host is one that is mirrored in our spiritual lives as well. Jesus came and lived a life that we could model. He emptied Himself of His Godhood and walked the Earth as a man to show how life could be lived. It is an absolutely explosive truth. He lived His life on earth abiding with the Father, in part, to give us a guide and example to follow. You can see this clearly in one of His final prayers in the book of John, often titled, "Jesus Prays for All Believers."

> **John 17:20-26** - "My prayer is not for them alone. I pray also for those who will believe in me through their message, that all of them may be one, Father, just as you are in me and I am in you. May they also be in us so that the world may believe that you have sent Me. I have given them the glory that you gave me, *that they may*

be one as we are one— I in them and you in me—so that they may be brought to complete unity. Then the world will know that you sent me and have loved them even as you have loved me.

All I have is yours, and all you have is mine. And glory has come to me through them. I will remain in the world no longer, but they are still in the world, and I am coming to you. Holy Father, protect them by the power of your name, the name you gave me, *so that they may be one as we are one"* (Emphasis added).

It isn't always easy being a good guest and a good host. It takes intentional effort and a value system to guide your actions. When it is done right, the result is abiding well with those around you. What is odd though is that we rarely, if ever, give much deep thought to that in terms of our relationship with God. He lives in us. Are we a good host for Him? Is He a good guest? And what of those moments when we are to dwell with Him? Is He a good host and are we a good guest? There is such a thin line between hospitality and hostility that it is worth thinking through.

If you thought about the very best of experiences as a host and as a guest and tried to put those into a set of guidelines what would they be? Scripture gives us a few snapshots, but there is one I would like us to focus on from Luke's gospel.

Luke 7:36-50 – "When one of the Pharisees invited Jesus to have dinner with him, He went to the Pharisee's house and reclined at the table. A woman in that town who lived a sinful life learned that Jesus was eating at the Pharisee's house, so she came there with an alabaster jar of perfume. As she stood behind Him at his feet weeping, she began to wet His feet with her tears. Then she wiped them with her hair, kissed them and poured perfume on them. When the Pharisee who had invited him saw this, he said to himself, 'If this man were a prophet, he would know who is touching him and what kind of woman she is—that she is a sinner.' Jesus answered him, 'Simon, I have something to tell you.' 'Tell me, teacher,' he said. 'Two people owed money to a certain moneylender. One owed him five hundred denarii, and the other fifty. Neither of them had the money to pay him back, so he forgave the debts of both. Now which of them will love him more?'

Simon replied, 'I suppose the one who had the bigger debt forgiven.' 'You have judged correctly,' Jesus said. Then he turned toward the woman and said to Simon, 'Do you see this woman? I came into your house. *You did not give me any water for my feet, but she wet my feet with her tears and wiped them with her hair. You did not give me a kiss, but this woman, from the time I entered, has not stopped kissing my feet. You did not put oil on my head, but she has poured perfume on my feet.* Therefore, I tell you, her many sins have been forgiven—as her great love has shown. But whoever has been forgiven little loves little.' Then Jesus said to her, 'Your sins are forgiven.' The other guests began to say among themselves, 'Who is this who even forgives sins?' Jesus said to the woman, 'Your faith has saved you; go in peace" *(Emphasis added)*.

There are a couple of key points that can be brought out from this as Jesus defined in part what hospitality means. The first principle is the act of washing another's feet. Transportation in the time of Jesus was a dirty and dusty thing. Most people didn't have horses to use for riding, so walking was the primary method of transportation. The roads weren't paved, and in arid climates the ground contained the remnants of everything that had passed through and been dropped in the area.

I got a firsthand lesson in this while I served in the Army. As part of that service I deployed to Kuwait for Operation Iraqi Freedom. I traveled all around the country working on my mission. Everyone over there had a low grade sinus infection for their entire deployment. There was so much dust in the air and you breathed it in constantly. One day as I was traveling I came upon the remains of a dead camel out in the open. It wasn't rotting, there wasn't enough rain for that, it was simply being sand blasted into oblivion. In a disturbing moment, it occurred to me that the wind was carrying little bits of dead camel everywhere and that was what I was breathing in. No wonder I had issues!

When sand storms would approach our base camps, it brought a type of gloom to the sky that was hard to imagine before I experienced it. It just seemed to suck the joy right out of us. One night a sandstorm raged. We woke up the next morning, and everything was covered with an eighth inch of dust. What a miserable night's sleep! It took a lot of time and effort to get rid of that. It was everywhere.

Even today, even though we have roads, sidewalks and the like, it still takes time to get rid of the metaphorical dirt we accumulate through the day. In the times of Jesus, as a proper host, it was their duty to help the guest get rid of that. It is a principle worth emulating.

What does it mean to do that well today? When my mother in law Judy comes down to see us from Lima, Ohio there is inevitably a time where we are talking about her trip. How was traffic? How was the bridge through Cincinnati? In a very real way we are "washing the dust off of her feet" when we have that conversation. It is a time in which we help her process the experiences she has gone through. It is the mark of a good host and a good relationship to help someone do that. It is a mark of a good guest to be open enough to share those experiences with the host.

For us to abide well with God, we have to do the same thing. He wants to hear about our day. He wants to help us process the experiences we have had. The work of Jesus on the cross is the ultimate washing because that removes our sins from the equation, but it doesn't end there. The way we process the experiences we have shapes us more and more every day into the likeness of Jesus.

How about the reverse though? It may seem like an unnecessary step, but if we are to be a good host to God, what does it mean for us to "wash the feet" of the Holy Spirit that lives within us? I think in a practical sense it is as simple as asking God how His day has been? Our prayers are often times dominated with the legitimate concerns we have, but we rarely ask God about what concerns Him? What did we miss? Who needs our prayers and our practical help? Taking the time to answer and ask those questions is the key to the first principle of being a good host and guest. This is part of what it means to abide.

When this is done well, we feel understood and loved, as do the people around us. There is nothing quite like stepping into someone else's world to help them feel that. Despite all the ways we fail, the God who made us and knows us is still around to talk to us, to help us process the world around us. It's just one of the ways He loves us.

The second principle deals with the signs of affection, kisses, and the anointing of oil. Anointing of oil is symbolic of many things in the Bible, but in the context of hospitality, really what we are talking about is whether we feel the guest is important and valued. Is that person worth honoring? Our affection and the value we place on our guest can be broken down into one simple question – are you happy to have them?

God is so happy to have us. As I mentioned before with my son, I came to a heightened sense of how great it was to see him once he left for college.

Every call, ever visit, every conversation – even the difficult ones – are special. So it bears repeating, He loves to spend time with His children. The follow on question then is are we happy to be His guest? There is a similar theme when we are the host. God is glad to come. Are we glad to see Him?

There are times we most certainly are. In times of trouble we show up to God's house, soaked in turmoil, dripping with the overflow of our bad decisions, and we exclaim – "I'm so glad your home! Do I ever need some help!" Whatever the circumstance, He is glad to see us. There is nothing wrong with that. It only becomes a problem when that is the _only_ time we come.

Do we remember to dwell with Him in the good times in our lives? Are we willing to bring Him as our guest into every facet of our lives? Often times when guests come over to my home, especially if we are in a hurry, one of the rooms in our homes becomes the sacrificial dumping ground of all the things we don't know what to do with. We just are going to pretend that room doesn't exist when we show people our house. Nope, not going there. As we invite God into our lives, being glad to see Him means being glad to have Him in all of the places in our lives; our work, our relationships, our bedrooms, our finances, our entertainment and certainly our speech.

> **Ephesians 4:29-32 (NLT):** "Do not use foul or abusive language. Let everything you say be good and helpful, so that your words will be an encouragement to those who hear them. _And do not bring sorrow to God's Holy Spirit by the way you live._ Remember, he has identified you as his own, guaranteeing that you will be saved on the day of redemption. Get rid of all bitterness, rage, anger, harsh words, and slander, as well as all types of evil behavior. Instead, be kind to each other, tenderhearted, forgiving one another, just as God through Christ has forgiven you" _(Emphasis added)._

Living obedient lives has as much to do with our witness to others as it is being a good host for the Holy Spirit in us. Those go hand in hand. Inconsistencies between our values and actions create tension. As a practical example, if you had guests over to your home to watch a big game, would you wear a jersey of the opposing team they cheer for? How awkward would that be? By living a life consistent with God's values we make our home His home. Having the right posture and being glad to have Him in every area of our lives is key to the second principle of abiding well.

When we do each of those, there isn't anywhere in the world we don't feel God is honored and welcome to be along with us. It guides our choices so that He is valued and cherished in every place of our lives.

Being a good guest and a good host to the Holy Spirit is the journey of a lifetime. I will never do it perfectly, but the rewards that come with the relationship make it impossible to pass up on the invitation.

For Further Reflection...

1.   What does it mean to be a good host?

2.   What does it mean to be a good guest?

3.   What is the tougher reality to work through: God living in your house, or you living in God's house?

4.   What are some of the ways we can practically wash the feet of one another in modern times?

5.   How do we show God we are glad to see Him?

6.   What are the toughest places to invite God along with us?

CHAPTER 13

Our Safe Space

God is spirit, and His worshipers must worship in the Spirit and in truth.

John 4:24

WHEN HAVE YOU HAD BUYER'S REMORSE? THAT TIME WHEN YOU bought something, it was delivered to you and it wasn't even close to what you thought you were getting. The internet is full of examples of this. It might be a dress from China that is nowhere near as elegant as advertised or furniture that is much smaller than the picture seemed to indicate. As funny as they might be to us, all of these kinds of things lead to disappointment.

I have a tick about me that when I sell something, especially something big, I tend to overshare about it. Like it is almost a phobia that I will be found to have tricked someone and they will think I am a fraud. I can't stand the idea.

When I graduated from college and I became an officer in the Army it was finally time for me to upgrade my car. At the time (1996) I was driving a 1982 Toyota Tercel. The car had definitely served me well, but it was WAY past its time. The front right quarter panel was dented heavily, there were spots of rust on it (somewhat hidden by the burnt orange paint color), and it felt like the engine was being held together with bailing wire and bubble gum. It was a mess. The thing was, from certain angles the car still looked pretty good. There wasn't much rust, I kept the car clean and waxed, and I put a product on the tires that made them shine.

When it came time to get my next car I began negotiating with the dealer. When it came to trade in value he asked how much I wanted for my current car. The advertisement for their dealer was that all vehicles had a minimum $500 trade in value. That was what I asked for. He furrowed his brow, asked me if I was sure, and when I replied in the positive, we proceeded with the deal.

The car I was buying needed to be serviced and cleaned, so we made an appointment to do the exchange of cars the following day. I had a friend of mine follow me to the dealer just to make sure if the car broke down on the way (a very real possibility) we would still get there. When I arrived I got my agent and we walked out to my old car. We approached it from the good side and as we walked up his eyebrows raised and he looked at me and said, "I might have got you on this one. This car looks like it is worth way more than $500." Then he circled the car. Then he opened the hood. Then he looked at the tires. Then he understood. Nope, he didn't get more than he bargained for, in fact, he might have gotten less.

Do you think God ever views you that way? After you have failed the thing you swore you would never fail again? When the anger comes back. When the addiction rears its ugly head. When the worry and fear returns. It is a far easier trap to fall into than you might think: that somehow God is disappointed in you. Like God purchased you on the cross but when He got you home he suddenly realized that your tires needed replaced. If He had only known!

If you ever feel that way know it is an absolute lie and nothing but pure garbage. God knew everything about you before He ever went to the cross.

And you know what? He still went. He doesn't have buyer's remorse now and He never will. Even on your worst day.

> **Romans 5:6-8:** "You see, at just the right time, when we were still powerless, Christ died for the ungodly. Very rarely will anyone die for a righteous person, though for a good person someone might possibly dare to die. But God demonstrates His own love for us in this: While we were still sinners, Christ died for us."

There is something truly freeing about this thought. The fact that God knew every dark and disturbing thing about you before He sacrificed for you proves the love that God feels for you. The value of the object you buy is proven by the price you are willing to pay. He bought you with the life of His son Jesus.

Jesus lived a life like ours. He was tempted in every way but He didn't sin.[14] He understands us and our struggles. He wants to help us through each of those. One of the ways He does that is through our act of confession.

Confession is one of the great liturgies of the Church. Jesus taught us to confess our sins in The Lord's Prayer (Matthew 6:12, NLT): "And forgive us our sins, as we have forgiven those who sin against us." Have you ever stopped to ask yourself why God wants us to do this? Confession literally means "to agree with." We are agreeing with God about something He already knows.

Given what we have established about God and His love for us, does it make sense to you that God would ask us to bring up our sins so He could scold and shame us? Maybe He wants to use this as an opportunity to ram it down our throats that we are so lucky to have Him, but if we screw up one more time, that's it! He's done with us! Does any of that sound consistent with a loving father? Of course it doesn't. Especially when you consider He knew it all before Jesus went to the cross.

So why is confession important and why do it? One valuable aspect of confession is that at the end of it we are still accepted. God sees everything we did, and guess what? He still loves us. Honestly and reciprocated acceptance of who another person is fuels intimacy. Our relationships may start with the mutual admiration of strengths, but it is the loving acceptance of weakness that fuels intimacy. He knows everything about us, and He accepts us as we are. We know next to nothing about Him, and He is offering us a chance to know Him. (We sometimes get those two mixed up and act like those facts are reversed.)

There is another key to confession that is critical to understand. We must be authentic.

1 John 1:8-9: "If we claim to be without sin, we deceive ourselves and the truth is not in us. If we confess our sins, He is faithful and just and will forgive us our sins and purify us from all unrighteousness."

This theme of authenticity is played out over and over throughout the Bible. One of those examples is contained in the book of Job. At the end of the book there is a curious line that God says to Eliphaz the Temanite. "After the Lord had said these things to Job, he said to Eliphaz the Temanite, "I am angry with you and your two friends, because you have not spoken the truth about me, as my servant Job has"" (Job 42:7).

Curiously, as we rewind through the Book of Job it is clear that Job said some things that he felt which were clearly wrong about God's character.

> **Job 9:16-18:** "Even if I summoned Him and He responded, I do not believe He would give me a hearing. He would crush me with a storm and multiply my wounds for no reason. He would not let me catch my breath but would overwhelm me with misery."

> **Job 10:3:** "Does it please You to oppress me, to spurn the work of your hands, while you smile on the plans of the wicked?"

So how do we reconcile the two? Do we think God forgot what Job said? It is far more likely that God was commending Job for coming to Him with his honest feelings and perceptions. He can deal with those emotions and questions about who He is. He is big enough to handle the questions.

We can also see this in the Psalms. The Psalms are full of passionate worship, prayers and observations from David and others, some of which are not exactly Godly. Far from teaching us that those emotions of violence and anger are okay, God is teaching us that it is okay for us to bring those emotions to Him.

> **Psalm 109:6-12:** "Appoint someone evil to oppose my enemy; let an accuser stand at his right hand. When he is tried, let him be found guilty, and may his prayers condemn him. May his days be few; may another take his place of leadership. May his children be fatherless and his wife a widow. May his children be wandering beggars; may they be driven from their ruined homes. May a creditor seize all he has; may strangers plunder the fruits of his labor. May no one extend kindness to him or take pity on his fatherless children."

It becomes hard to read after a while. It would take enormous theological twists and contortions to justify his emotions as Godly. They aren't. What the Psalms are trying to convey to us is not that these emotions are righteous, but that whatever emotions we have – sadness, joy, anger, and depression – they all can be brought to God who is willing to hear our cries. (And gentle reader, if you think I cherry picked the worst example I would refer you to Psalm 137.)

David wasn't perfect. He had spectacular victories and spectacular failures in his life. Yet even with the imperfections the description God said about David is repeated in Acts 13:22 that he was "a man after mine own heart". In part, that description is based upon the way that David came before God.

He came honestly and he came humbly. We can do the same, but we have to realize that those two traits come hand in hand. If we are being honest about ourselves and our weaknesses, it will induce the humility we need to approach God in the right way.

Only one man has ever been worthy of worship, and that is Jesus. Few people outside of that are worthy even of adoration. When we look at the men and women of the Bible we see the complications, the successes and failures, the humanness of each. It is one of the reasons I have faith that the Bible is true. The people in it are real, warts and all, just like us. It isn't a glossed over version that is sanitized to lead us to a conclusion. These are real people with real emotions dealing with a very real God. The people in the Bible aren't air brushed, but rather even the people who are the heroes have their faults. It is a beautiful love story from God to us, and when we come to Him honestly, He can help us and deal with us in a way that shapes us to become more like Him. We become part of that story.

When we approach God with honesty and humility it is safe space. Psychological safety is a much talked about term these recent days, but God has always had that in mind.

> **James 1:5:** "If any of you lacks wisdom, you should ask God, who gives generously to all without finding fault, and it will be given to you."

God is looking to give wisdom to us without finding fault. He is looking for us to come authentically to Him so He can give us wisdom and shape us into His likeness. In 2 Corinthians 10:5 states "We demolish arguments and every pretension that sets itself up against the knowledge of God, and we take captive every thought to make it obedient to Christ." The phrase "taking captive" it is a picture of taking a prisoner by spear point. In our lives we will often come up against thoughts and emotions that we can't get rid of and don't even know what to do with. In those times you can bring those thoughts and emotions before God and ask Him what He wants done with them.

Maybe it's a sanctified imagination, but as I pray into those moments where I have thoughts and emotions I can't seem to corral on my own, I will imagine holding a spear and me poking along the embodiment of those emotions or thoughts into the presence of God. We can ask God, the one who loves us more than anything else ever could, what should we do with these things? His response is never shame. His response is never condemnation. It is understanding, wisdom and love.

God will not bless your avatar – the image you want the world to believe you really are. God will not sanctify your selfie. When we are not acting the way we normally do around our best friends they know something is wrong. They can't help me unless I let them in and help them to understand what is really wrong. What is the tragedy in all of this is that God already knows what's wrong. He won't force His way in, so as long as we pretend that everything is okay, He can't do His work. Anyone who has been through counseling will tell you that for it to have any chance to be effective, all parties have to be honest about what has happened and how they feel. It is only when all of the broken pieces are put out on the table that there is a chance that it can be put back together.

To abide well is to come to God honestly. Let's bring Him everything. Bring Him our desires, our victories, our defeats. Bring Him our sin, our faith filled work, our doubts. Bring Him our love, our hate and even our apathies. He wants them all. He wants all of you. He paid the highest price imaginable for the thing He loves the most – you.

So come as you are. He loves you just as you are. He also loves you too much to let you remain in the things that aren't good for you. Those aren't mutually exclusive. God is the ultimate safe space to abide with and to work on those things with Him together.

For Further Reflection...

1. What does it mean to come to God honestly?

2. Why is that important?

3. Is God "safe space" to deal with your issues?

4. Is God "safe"?

5. What role does confession have in the relationships you have with the people around you?

6. Are there any emotions you can't bring to God?

CHAPTER 14

A Team of Misfits

*Just as a body, though one, has many parts, but all its
many parts form one body, so it is with Christ. For we
were all baptized by one Spirit so as to form one body—
whether Jews or Gentiles, slave or free—and we were all
given the one Spirit to drink. Even so the body is not made
up of one part but of many.*

1 Corinthians 12:12-14

I SERVED IN THE ARMY FOR JUST UNDER NINE YEARS AS AN ARMOR officer. I got to work with some absolutely amazing people during my time in the Army and I was blessed incredibly by it. One of the things you learn early on in your time in the Army is that everyone has a different role to play in the broader mission that has to be accomplished. Yes, you may have a specific role, and a specific goal, but that feeds into a larger mission that requires many different types of people to accomplish.

Infantry are essential to any mission because they are the physical people on the ground. In a very real way they influence or control the space they occupy. As with so many things in life, if you want to create change, you can't just send dollars, or for that matter, just your prayers, you have to send people. It begins with them.

They can't do it alone in combat though, or if they try, they can't do it for very long. They need the wise and often times better looking armor soldiers to help them (I just had to add that!) to complete their missions and to eliminate larger and better armed opponents.

All joking aside, the armor community certainly cannot do it by itself. One tank alone can burn up to four hundred gallons of fuel a day. A single tank! We cannot survive in the field long without significant support from the logistics professionals that are helping to sustain all of the combat soldiers on the front lines. There are many time more soldiers, government civilians, and contractors supporting combat then there are actual trigger pulling combat soldiers. That said, the way an army sustains itself in the field is incredibly complex. There is a quote, often attributed to General Omar Bradley (one of the greatest generals in World War II) that says, "Amateurs talk strategy, professionals talk logistics."

In every unit I was in there were rivalries. Everyone thought their aspect of the mission was the most important. There were, and continue to be, struggles for resources and emphasis in planning for future missions that highlight the capabilities of one part of the team or another. In the end the best units are ones that bring together a group of incomplete misfits into one team dedicated to one mission. They become complete as they work together, each in their area, with their eyes on the greater mission.

It may be that the greatest sin that anyone in the military can ever commit is to think, "I can do this by myself." It simply isn't true. To believe you are complete and whole by yourself is vanity; unfortunately, there may be no thought more American - a country that celebrates (and sometimes worships) the rugged individualist as an idol.

Selfishness in relationships is a fast acting poison that can be recognized quickly. Self-reliance is a slower moving poison that stunts growth and maturity, and eventually prevents goals from being accomplished. It is every bit as deadly.

1 COR 12:15-31: "Now if the foot should say, 'Because I am not a hand, I do not belong to the body,' it would not for that reason stop being part of the body. And if the ear should say, 'Because I am not an eye, I do not belong to the body,' it would not for that reason stop being part of the body. *If the whole body were an eye, where would the sense of hearing be? If the whole body were an ear, where would the sense of smell be? But in fact God has placed the parts in the body, every one of them, just as he wanted them to be. If they were all one part, where would the body be? As it is, there are many parts, but one body.*

The eye cannot say to the hand, 'I don't need you!' And the head cannot say to the feet, 'I don't need you!' On the contrary, those parts of the body that seem to be weaker are indispensable, and the parts that we think are less honorable we treat with special honor. And the parts that are unpresentable are treated with special modesty, while our presentable parts need no special treatment. But God has put the body together, giving greater honor to the parts that lacked it, so that there should be no division in the body, but that its parts should have equal concern for each other. *If one part suffers, every part suffers with it; if one part is honored, every part rejoices with it.*

> Now you are the body of Christ, and each one of you is a part of it. And God has placed in the church first of all apostles, second prophets, third teachers, then miracles, then gifts of healing, of helping, of guidance, and of different kinds of tongues. Are all apostles? Are all prophets? Are all teachers? Do all work miracles? Do all have gifts of healing? Do all speak in tongues? Do all interpret? Now eagerly desire the greater gifts" *(Emphasis added)*.

God placed in each of us His Spirit, skills, and abilities that the greater body needs. None of us has it all. None of us have all of the gifts – we aren't meant to. By being different God has emphasized unity as a way of achieving "on Earth as it is in Heaven."[15]

A key piece to abiding in Christ is abiding with one another. Self-sufficiency cuts off the Christ in others that we desperately need. Abiding with Christ by abiding with other believers transforms us from a group of incomplete misfits into one team dedicated to one mission.

This is FAR easier said than done. One of the most difficult things to do is to accept wisdom from someone who is different than you, or for that matter just plain annoys you. It happens over and over again in my life. They might be someone from a different political party. They might be a different culture or economic background. They might be that overly cheerful morning person at your office. They might be a grumpy curmudgeon that might as well have taken the character Eeyore as their personal hero. It might even be your spouse. (Gentle reader, if you have been married more than a day you already know what I mean.) In each case the Christ in them seems to come out in the most inopportune times – namely when I need them the most.

I have to swallow hard and I have to access humility in my life. For some of us that isn't an easy thing to do. (Most of us really.) The wisdom that comes from those moments may be the thing that propels us to greater achievements, all for God's glory. To ignore them or to control your environment so that you don't come into contact with those people is to turn your back on abiding with Christ through His body.

Self-sufficiency has another terrible effect in that as you become more self-sufficient service to others becomes harder and harder. We are as intimate as we are dependent on each other. To put it another way, when we lose a sense of dependency on each other then we lose the intimacy necessary to deeply abide with one another.

My dog Oreo has an amazing ability. He can recognize when I have completed all my tasks for the day and have just sat down in my chair to relax and maybe watch a little television. It is at that moment when I have gotten most comfortable in my chair, secure in all that I needed to get done, that our dog hits his paws on the door chimes, signaling it needs to go outside. It is uncanny.

I have a choice to make that that point. I can ignore the dogs call and risk a mess in the house, or I can get up and open the door. I often times shake my head. It would have been so much easier to have done this while I was still up and doing other things. Why did the dog have to wait until now? We do it though, because we care for our pets, and we certainly don't want the mess.

That choice doesn't only apply to our pets. Ever had your spouse ask you to do something at the end of your day? Ever had friend come into need at a less than opportune time? The very goal of self-sufficiency insulates us from serving others when they need it. That intimacy can save us when we are in trouble later on down the road. When we weave together strings into one rope the whole becomes stronger than the sum of the individual strings. We can handle more weight together. To abide in Christ by abiding with each other enables us to be more than the sum of our individual parts.

When we consider the earlier passages in 1 Corinthians 12, the funny thing is that unity with each other and spiritual gifts (another kind of fruit and a subject for a different day), lead us to a very specific thing. It is important to remember than when the books of the Bible were written, they didn't have chapters or verses numbered. They read as a continuous flow. So what comes right after 1 Corinthians 12? One of the greatest verses on love you will ever read.

> **1 COR 13:1-8:** "If I speak in the tongues of men or of angels, but do not have love, I am only a resounding gong or a clanging cymbal. If I have the gift of prophecy and can fathom all mysteries and all knowledge, and if I have a faith that can move mountains, but do not have love, I am nothing. If I give all I possess to the poor and give over my body to hardship that I may boast, but do not have love, I gain nothing.

> Love is patient, love is kind. It does not envy, it does not boast, it is not proud. It does not dishonor others, it is not self-seeking, it is not easily angered, it keeps no record of wrongs. Love does not delight in evil but rejoices with the truth. It always protects, always trusts, always hopes, always perseveres.

> Love never fails"

So now we have come full circle. We began with love and saw how serving other people was a key aspect of the fruit. Now we have seen that as we serve those people we abide with Christ in them, which in turn allows us to product more fruit. Each aspect of the fruit feeds into how we abide. Each aspect of how we abide feeds into how we produce fruit. It is an ascending circle that leads us to know God in ways we could hardly begin to imagine.

Jump in anywhere you like, it will bring you back to Him, it brings us back to each other, and it will bring you back to love.

For Further Reflection...

1. What does it mean to abide?

2. Why doesn't God give all of the gifts to one person?

3. What is so corrosive about being self-sufficient?

4. Is self-sufficiency all bad? When does it become so?

5. Can you truly become intimate with someone without being dependent in some way?

6. What are some of the most challenging aspects of abiding with others in Christ?

7. What are the greatest benefits of abiding with others in Christ?

8. What practical steps can you take to do so more often?

CHAPTER 15

Final Thoughts

Whether you turn to the right or to the left, your ears will hear a voice behind you, saying, "This is the way; walk in it."

Isaiah 30:21

ONE OF MY OFF AND ON AGAIN HOBBIES IS GEOCACHING: AN ACTIVity where you go out into the world and find things that others have hidden for you to discover. It uses a website where people log geocaches (or sometimes just known as caches) into a database and then you use a GPS to go find them.

The cache that you go out and find can be large or very small. It can be very well hidden or, relatively speaking, out in the open. The terrain you traverse can be very challenging, or it might be as simple as stepping out of your car.

I love to hike, so this adds a bit of adventure to the places I go. I've found over a thousand of them over the years. Some of the way the caches are hidden are incredibly clever. I've even hidden a few myself. Just a really good time that has brought some joy to hikes I have taken with friends. On a certain level, it is a little absurd, and I get that. There is an old joke in geocaching that goes – Geocaching: We use billion dollar satellites to find Tupperware hidden in the woods. It's a fun time though and you should try it.

The app even has a compass function so that you can figure out where you need to go. It uses the GPS in your phone, compares the place you are to where you need to go, and then gives you a direction.

Many times you follow the compass through woods, over hills, up the sides of mountains, and I've crossed a stream or two. My wife would tell you that the muddier I was when I returned from going geocaching the happier I seemed to be.

At a certain point, a funny thing happens. When you are traveling, the compass starts to spin. First it might be north, then south, then as you wander, it might be west, then to the east. What is happening? There are two distinct possibilities.

The first possibility is that your compass might be broken. This has happened a time or two with me. I've closed the app, powered down my phone, and restarted all of the programs. That has worked more than once for me. It always helps when you are getting the right signals.

The second possibility comes when you trust the compass and the directions you are being given. Then it might be that the compass is spinning because you have reached your destination. At that point it is time to stop paying attention to the compass and to start observing the world around you. It is where you realize that something out there in the world has been hidden for you, and now instead of a compass, you need focused eyes to see.

Yes, there might be other possible reasons, but those two cover about 95% of the instances in my experience.

Our walk with God can be much the same way. At least in my life there have been times where I felt like I got clear direction from God. I felt a clear path was placed in front of me, and when I spoke to other wise believers they confirmed that it was consistent with Scripture and God's heart for me. There is an excitement that comes with the clarity of knowing where you are going and what you are supposed to be doing. There are people I know who absolutely live for that feeling. Once they know they are on the right path with what God wants them to do in their lives, watch out – nothing will stop them.

Then there are other times. Times that are less clear. Times where the compass seems to be spinning. Sometimes you think you have a clear path ahead and then all of the sudden it seems like the opposite is now the truth. These can be some of the most frustrating times in our lives where clear direction doesn't seem to be coming to us. What should we do in these situations?

In much the same way as with geocaching, I think there are two distinct possibilities that cover a lot of the scenarios we face in our lives.

The first is that, indeed, your compass might be broken. God continues to speak to us today, but sometimes it is our ability to hear Him that is the issue. Sin in our life tends to deaden our hearing. In a spiritual sense our hearing is very focus based. (If you ask my wife she might argue the same is true in the natural world as well.) If you aren't focusing on God with how you live your life, then you may very well have trouble hearing from Him. As we talked about in the previous chapter, this is a key feature in abiding with God. Obedience to Him and His word is exceptionally important if we are to hear clearly.

And while perfection is certainly not required for God to speak to us, it may be that God has to work something out of our lives before we can move onto something else. So if you don't feel you are hearing from God, it is worth praying about. It may be that there is something you need to leave behind or it may simply be that He gave you direction earlier and He is waiting on you to do that before He gives you the next set of directions. I've had each of those occur in my life.

The really intriguing thing that I would like to focus on is the second possibility that might exist. It might just be that you have reached your destination.

One of the terms people often use when talking about economically poor and underserved areas is food desert. This refers to an area that has limited or no access to affordable and nutritious food. People who live in these areas have been found to be at higher risks for diet related conditions, such as obesity, diabetes and cardiovascular disease. It could be a low income area or it could be that the people living there have to travel much farther to find a healthy option.

I think the same thing exists in the spiritual sense. There are places and people out there who are starved for the fruit of the Spirit. There are symptoms in the natural for a food desert and there are symptoms in the spiritual.

> **Galatians 5: 19-21:** "The acts of the flesh are obvious: sexual immorality, impurity and debauchery; idolatry and witchcraft; *hatred, discord, jealousy, fits of rage, selfish ambition, dissensions, factions and envy;* drunkenness, orgies, and the like. I warn you, as I did before, that those who live like this will not inherit the kingdom of God" *(Emphasis added).*

Those highlighted attributes might as well be a role call for what we see in our communities and nation, not to mention the nightly news. So to expand on the thought above, it may not only be that as the compass spins you have reached your destination, but that you have found a place you need to set up a fruit stand. The world has never needed it more.

When you look up, who around you needs patience? Who around you needs kindness? Who around you needs love in one form or another? There are so many possibilities that are out there and so many needs. As we lift our eyes out of our Bibles and look for practical ways to serve, we will discover that the fruit God is producing in us is desperately needed by those around us.

And don't mistake what I mean when I say to lift our eyes out of our Bibles. In so many ways our Bibles act as a practical compass as we relate to God in our everyday lives. To ignore it is to invite destruction into our lives, but it can't be the only thing we look at. Our relationship with God, developed in prayer and by study of the Word, feeds our service to others. Our service to others in turn feeds our relationship with God, deepening and strengthening it.

The truth is that the sick and the suffering are all around us, some just hide it better than others. Some live in countries far away, some live in your community, and some may even live in your home. Malnourished and starving, they need what you have been given to help them be the person God made them to be.

What an incredible gift we have been given to have relationship with God and others. What an incredible privilege we have been given to serve God and others. The full circle of relationship, abiding, and producing fruit that then deepens relationship is the path to victory in whatever faces us.

We have been given a mission. The phrase "on Earth as it is in Heaven", given to us in Matthew 6:10, wasn't a prayer given to us to keep us busy until Christ returned. It also didn't come without the resources to achieve it if we are willing to trust in Him. It doesn't come automatically though. For that, we must choose to produce fruit, and we must choose to abide.

Romans 15:18-19 states: "I will not venture to speak of anything except what Christ has accomplished through me in leading the Gentiles to obey God by what I have said and done – by the power of signs and wonders, through the power of the Spirit of God." There are times we think of "signs and wonders" as only magnificent acts of parting the Red Sea or raising someone from the dead, but as an example I believe that an act of patience in the face of terrible hostility is no less a miracle and can change the course of history. I think most people if you asked them would believe the science fiction paradigm that if you went back in time and changed one small thing it could have enormous consequences to the future. Few of us seem to believe that in the present a small act of kindness, patience or love could radically change the future. The reality is that people are changed and brought to Christ by the fruit we produce. That is truly powerful.

Acts 4:13 states: "When they saw the courage of Peter and John and realized they were unschooled, ordinary men, they were astonished and they took note that these men had been with Jesus." That courage was a combination of peace and self-control that came out of abiding. When people see you displaying the fruit of the Spirit in difficult situations they will know that you have been with Jesus. They may not articulate it that way, but they will know something is different and special within you, and that is the gateway to a great conversation. As we produce fruit, God is glorified.

> **John 15:8:** "This to my Father's glory, that you bear much fruit, showing yourselves to be my disciples."

There is such treasure that awaits us if we do this well. It is a declarative statement. If we abide, we will produce fruit. The fruit must be harvested, protected and given (our responsibilities) but the production is His. It is a balance, a partnership and the greatest relationship we can ever invest in. It is the journey to a more fruitful life.

So with that, it's now time to take what we have learned and get to work. As we begin that journey, it seems appropriate for me to close this book as we began it. With a simple prayer over us both.

Lord God, let us be one with you, so that we may bear much fruit. Let us serve others, see Your goodness in the land of the living, and let others see it fully in us. Amen.

Thanks

As with any monumental endeavor, there are so many people to say thank you to. Janay Sutton, Brother Shawn Edwards, and Dr. Daryl Pepper all made significant contributions to the editing of the material you have before you. They corrected and encouraged me and made the book so much more than it was. I am truly thankful to each.

Seth and Haley Anderson, Bob Bivens, Jenny Crippen, Sharon and Lloyd Fish, Angela and Scott Humphrey, Rachel Hunter, Glenda Irwin, Nancy Lennon, Marilee Loftus, Sherry Malito, and Kurt Peterson completed a run through of the material during fall classes at Grace Heartland Church. They provided additional insights, corrections, and helped me to refine the material and questions as we went along. They were a joy to have in class and their learning encouraged me more than I can say.

The run through also provided space for additional learning about these important topics. Brother Shawn Edwards's suggestion and the willingness of my home church to allow me to run through the material was a gift that made the book so much better. I am thankful for each and every one of the staff at Grace Heartland who do such an amazing job at modeling the love of Christ to so many.

Finally I would like to thank my family who put up with the time away I spent on this project. I am so thankful for their love and encouragement.

Endnotes

1. Jadev Payeng: The Man Who Planted an Entire Forest by Himself, Interesting Engineering, Susan Fourtane, 11 SEP 2018 (Page 4)

2. Proverbs 22:8, Psalm 126:5-6, 2 COR 9:6-8, Galatians 6:7-10 (Page 14)

3. Proverbs 18:9, James 4:17 (Page 20)

4. Hebrews 4:15 (Page 30)

5. Colossians 2 (Page 57)

6. What Makes Online Content Viral, Jonah Berger, Katherine Milkman, 1 APR 2012 (Page 58)

7. Matthew 5:43-48 (Page 73)

8. Definition, Oxford Dictionary On-Line, www.lexico.com (Page 77)

9. Deuteronomy 31:6, Hebrews 13:5 (Page 95)

10. Definition, HELPS Word-Studies, BibleHub.com (Page 101)

11. Down in Green Pastures; He Leads Me beside Still Waters, Michael G. McKelvey. Tabletalkmagazine.com. August 2018 (Page 132)

12. Definition, HELPS Word-Studies, BibleHub.com (Page 135)

About The Author

Jason Root has proudly served as an officer in the Army, as a Project, Resident and Area Engineer in the Corps of Engineers, and now as the Director of Public Works for Fort Knox. He worships and serves at Grace Heartland Church in Elizabethtown, Kentucky. He holds a Bachelor of Science in Civil Engineering from The Ohio State University. When he isn't traveling across the country to watch his son play or coach basketball he can be found hiking, kayaking, or volunteering in his church and community. He lives in Elizabethtown with his wife, Beth, and his dog, Oreo.